A Commentary on
PHILIPPIANS

UNLOCKING THE NEW TESTAMENT

A Commentary on
PHILIPPIANS

David Pawson

Anchor Recordings

First published in Great Britain in 2017 by
Anchor Recordings Ltd
DPTT, Synegis House, 21 Crockhamwell Road,
Woodley, Reading RG5 3LE

**For more of David Pawson's teaching,
including DVDs and CDs, go to
www.davidpawson.com**

**FOR FREE DOWNLOADS
www.davidpawson.org**

**For further information, email
info@davidpawsonministry.org**

ISBN 978 1 909886 74 2

Printed by Lightning Source

Contents

This book is based on a series of talks. Originating as it does from the spoken word, its style will be found by many readers to be somewhat different from my usual written style. It is hoped that this will not detract from the substance of the biblical teaching found here.

As always, I ask the reader to compare everything I say or write with what is written in the Bible and, if at any point a conflict is found, always to rely upon the clear teaching of scripture.

David Pawson

Please read Philippians 1:1–11

The Romans established a colony at Philippi, realising its strategic significance. But God is a strategist as well, and he had his eye on that city too, and he wanted a colony of heaven in there so that everybody going from Europe to Asia would have to pass through *his* colony. He knew exactly the man to bring: Paul.

The way in which Paul was brought to Philippi was extraordinary. Notice that he was guided because he was on the move. Do you know it takes very little pressure to change the direction of a moving body, but it takes a lot of power to change the direction of a static one? Try turning the steering wheel of your car while it is stationary and then try turning it when it is moving. God has difficulty moving static people in a different direction. He would much rather people were moving in the wrong direction and he can correct them rather than their sitting still and saying, "I'm scared to move in case I go the wrong way." That is why one of the oft-quoted texts about guidance is, "You will hear a voice behind you say, 'This is the way, walk in it, don't turn to the right, don't turn to the left.'" We ignore the most crucial word there, which is "behind". We say, "Lord, please give us a voice in front – we're scared to move in case we go the wrong way."

The Bible teaches: You get moving, you step out, and if you are going the wrong way you will hear a voice behind you, saying, "Get back in the way."

So Paul was not sitting and saying, "Please Lord, where

do I go next?" Off he went toward Asia and he heard a voice behind him, re-directing his steps. So he kept on moving, came to Troas and then took the boat across the sea.

I want to plead with you not to be afraid to make mistakes. The person who never makes mistakes never makes anything. The voice comes behind you as you step out in faith, according to all the light you have. Step out that way and let God speak from behind and say, "You're turning right" or "you're turning left" – a very important principle of guidance – rather than sitting and waiting. When he was forbidden to go to Asia or Bithynia, Paul did not run back to where he was and say, "I went wrong, let's go back there and sit still and wait." He went on and the Lord closed door after door so that he could open the one at the end of the corridor, and the gospel came to Europe.

The church in Philippi was an extraordinary mixture. The first three prominent members were: a wealthy Asian businesswoman; a slave girl who was a clairvoyant, and a Roman non-commissioned officer. Would you have put those three together and said, "Now we can have a fellowship"? Only God would think of doing such a thing. God wanted variety and unity in his church.

This church was not suffering from doctrinal error, so Paul did not come with a heavy hand. He had to at Corinth, but not here. Nor was there ethical perversion in the church at Philippi. So he did not have to rebuke someone strongly as at Corinth. The only problem he was concerned about with this church, with which he had such a lovely relationship, was their unity. There were tensions. Two ladies, Euodia and Syntyche, were getting a little out of touch with each other. Then there was also a sense that the members were standing on their rights. Paul had to point out that Jesus, who was equal with God, did not stand on his rights. He was going to be a servant, obedient to death.

The first eleven verses of this letter are no more than the conventional opening of any letter written two thousand years ago. They didn't use envelopes, they used a long piece of paper, wrote on it and rolled it up. So the first bit that was unrolled was the beginning, and it was there that they very sensibly wrote the name of the sender, the address, and the person it was going to, a formal greeting, and that was usually followed with some kind of a wish, like our "Hope you are well, wish you were here" – very conventional and understandable. That was better than our custom of putting the name of the sender at the end, particularly if the letter is a long one.

Paul could not just say, "From Paul to the people at Philippi – Hello, wish you were here, hope you're well." No, he had to pack it with his own unique touch. It is an example of how Christians can touch the ordinary and make it extraordinary, how they can take a natural thing and make it supernatural, so touching life that everything they do is shot through with the dimension that you hear nowhere else.

Let us look at the address first and then that little original greeting. The address is from Paul *and* Timothy. I draw your attention to four pairs here. First of all, there are a couple of names, yet the letter is clearly from one. That is amazing. If I judge Paul's temperament rightly, he was a bit of an individualist, a loner, and here he is again and again in a beautiful way associating somebody else with him. These two names are so opposite that you would have said, "No, I'd never put those together to work as a team." Here is Paul, a driving man with tremendous ambition, a very strong personality, a real go-getter, and here is Timothy, a rather shy, timid young man who often has stomach trouble and needs to take a little wine for it. Who would have taken Paul and Timothy and said, "You are going to make a good team"? Yet the Holy Spirit has taken them and put them so together that when Paul sends a letter he can say, "This is from both of us." If you study the church's history at Philippi you will find that both contributed to that church. How important it is for a church not to depend on the ministry of one man. That is an issue that makes many pastors feel threatened. But I can tell you what happens if you depend on one man: you get cliques: "I'm of Paul," "I'm of Apollos," "I'm of Cephas," "I'm of David Pawson," or of someone else.... Now that is just not the church of Jesus Christ. We are going to see that there is a striking absence here of something we might have expected.

Here is another pair of words I want you to notice: "To the elders and deacons." Well, where's the pastor? What happened to him? Won't this go to the manse? The answer is no, there is no manse and there's no pastor. There are elders and deacons, both plural. I find no pattern in the New Testament that is not a *plurality* of leadership. The interesting thing is that elders and deacons are not ecclesiastical titles, they are not church status symbols, they are words taken from the political sphere, from the religious sphere, from the social sphere of the ancient world. Any community that was banded together for any purpose needed two sorts of people to help it along. They needed leaders who would be foremen, superintendents of the work, whether it was a church or a political society or whatever. They also needed deacons, and the word means "helpers" or "servants", who would look after the money and the welfare of the community. Every community, no matter what you get together for, whether it is a squash club or political party or whatever, is going to have to have leaders to superintend and helpers to serve. The church is a community, so it comes as no surprise that the pattern which emerges in it is the normal pattern that is needed by any group of people: elders to superintend, deacons to serve.

The translations of the word "elder" or the Greek word *presbuteros* are so varied that we get into all kinds of titles. One translation is "bishop", but what does that word signify to you? A man with a purple shirt and a crook in his hand? It helps to understand the context in life of the Greek word. That term "bishop" was used on a building site in ancient Greece. If you arrived with a cart full of bricks and you said, "Where's the foreman?" they would reply, "Well, the bishop's in the hut down there." That is all it means. It means the foreman, the one who is called to superintend the work, to co-ordinate, to direct it, to say what is needed at a certain point. You get the helpers as well.

That is the pattern for every normal church: a plurality of leaders whose job it is to superintend the work and to shape it and direct, and a plurality of helpers whose job it is to see that all the practical things that are needed get done. But bear in mind that their primary function is not towards the building or a denomination, but towards the people of God. They are to superintend and serve them. That is the pattern of ministry in the New Testament. Within that broad pattern there are specific ministries – apostle, prophet, evangelist, pastor, teacher, and all the rest that can be recognised and used. But the basic pattern is those to lead and to supervise and those to serve – two functions needed in whatever community you have. So Paul doesn't mention the pastor because there isn't *one*. There were probably quite a number.

Here is the third pair of words. It says: From Paul and Timothy, *servants* of Christ Jesus, to the *saints* at Philippi. Isn't it amazing that we so change things around that most people today would say: this is the epistle of *Saint* Paul to the *servants* of God at Philippi. But Paul doesn't say that. This is the epistle of servant Paul to the saints. It is the opposite of the way we think. Are you a saint? Isn't it marvellous to be a saint? Who canonised you? You are supposed to be dead and have performed two miracles through your bones and have had prayers offered to you and have them answered before you can be called "saint" in some branches of the church. I thank God that he says: David, you are a saint, now I've given you something to live up to, but in my mind you're a saint. What does this word "saint" mean? It does not mean a spiritual elite of very special people who have reached a degree of sanctification way above the ordinary. It means a person who has been set apart for God, at whom God can look and say, "He's mine", or, "She's mine." Of course that has implications for the way you live. A saint is someone who is different from other people because he or she is separated to God, *belongs to God* – and that should make a difference immediately.

The translators of the Authorized Version could not cope with this word. Paul often writes to the people at various places who are "... called saints" and the translators thought, "It can't mean that, it is pushing it a bit too far." So they slipped in two words that were never there in the original: "to be". But we are not *called to be* saints, we are *called saints*. Isn't that amazing? That is what provides the motivation to be saints: the fact that God calls you one and treats you as one.

The fourth pair of words is: "grace and peace". If you lived among Jews, you would say when meeting somebody "Peace" – *shalom*. It is a lovely word meaning harmony. It means harmony with yourself, so it means health. It means harmony with other people, so it means happiness. It means harmony with God, so it means holiness. It is a big word and it means everything that God wishes for you. But how can you get *shalom*? It is all very well to say to somebody, "I hope you'll have health, happiness and holiness," but how are they going to get it? Paul knew that you need something else before that: you need *grace*. You will never get peace until you have grace. You don't hear Israelis saying, "Grace and peace to you," but you hear them saying "Peace". Then if you study their poems, their art and literature, you find the one thing they haven't got is peace, because they have refused grace, and if you refuse grace you can't have peace. The word "grace" is very like a greeting used in the Greek world. When you met somebody you said something slightly different, "charine", which was similar to "charis". Paul took that word and filled it with meaning. "Grace" refers to what you receive but you don't deserve – that's all. God is so generous. He doesn't say: Does this person deserve this gift of mine? He just says: Will you receive it? That is grace. Once you are living in grace you will live in peace. These two go together.

Now to the greeting. The way Paul expresses this is a sermon in itself. Again it is using a convention to express something much more than good wishes. We are now shown how Paul prayed. It has been said that you learn more about someone from their praying than their preaching. I think it would help me to understand where you are spiritually if I could listen in on your private prayers. You would certainly know where I was if you could listen to mine. Paul is baring his heart, wanting the reader to see into his prayer life.

Christians don't *wish* each other anything. Somebody facing a real problem, a very young Christian, only a few weeks old, was feeling that God was calling them to face a very difficult situation and asked me whether they should. I said, "It's not for me to tell you, I think the Lord has already told you."

The person said, "Yes, I'm going to face it. Wish me luck as I face it, won't you?"

I said, "No, I won't. I don't believe in luck. There's no such thing as chance to the child of God, everything is ordered by divine providence. I'd like to give you a marvellous little book of Bible readings for each day so that you can hear God directing your path. Let's open it and see what it says." I opened it and read the first passage I set my eyes on, and it was the only passage in the Bible that specifically referred to the problem that person was facing. I continued, "Now do you believe there is no such thing as chance?" Statistically, the odds against that happening right there were enormous, but God had ordered it and he spoke his word into the situation. So it was not luck. You don't *wish* people well, you pray and you tell them what you are praying for.

Studying Paul's prayers, I saw three dimensions that are not present in natural human prayer. There is a profound difference between Christian prayer, and the prayer of other religions. The idea is going around that because we all pray that means we are all travelling different roads to the same goal, and that the Tibetan turning his prayer wheel and swinging it round is doing exactly the same thing as I do when I get on my knees. That is absolute rubbish. It is the framework and the content of prayer, not *whether* you pray, that makes you a Christian. Most people pray, I find, especially when they are in a difficult situation – it is natural to pray. An opinion poll found that although the vast majority in Britain do not go to church, most people claimed that they prayed. But does that make them Christians? Not in the slightest. Study the content of their prayer and you will find it totally different from Christian prayer. Anybody can pray the kind of slot machine prayer. "I've got a need, I'll put a prayer in and put my hand out and hope that the answer comes out." That is natural prayer.

Let us think about three dimensions of Christian prayer which make it quite different from anybody else's. First, a very simple truth: *say thank you before you say please.* Now that is not natural. Other people who pray always say "please" and they don't always say "thank you", but if they do, it comes later. Have you noticed that? Only Christians realise that when they come with an urgent need to God they have so much for which to say thank you first. A sacrifice of praise and thanksgiving invariably precedes requests in true Christian prayer.

So Paul does not start by saying, "I'm praying this, that and the other for you...." He says, "Thank God," and then later he says, "And this is what I ask for you. But whenever I pray for you my first response is: Thank you, thank you, thank you Lord!" Do you remember the ten lepers Jesus healed? He healed the lot. They wanted healing, "Please heal us," and he healed them. Only one came back and said thank you. But even if all ten had come back and said thank you, that would still not have been Christian prayer.

I remember one evangelistic crusade in which I was involved. I was then living in a caravan and it was just about the time I met my wife. We had an early morning prayer meeting in the caravan, and at first only one little lady came to it, and she was a dear saint. I will never forget this lesson: she not only said thank you for other things first, but she also said thank you for things she asked for before she got them. She would pray, "Lord, just do this tonight at the meeting," and then she would say, "Thank you Lord for doing it, thank you!" and she was looking forward to seeing the result of her thanks. That is real faith, a prayer of faith. Thankfulness is the thread of Christian prayer. The word "please" is natural; "thank you" is supernatural, especially when it comes first, especially when it comes before the world would say thank you. So here is the first simple point. Now he says, quite honestly, "Whenever I pray for you...." I want to make a plea that you never promise anyone what you will not fulfil in terms of prayer. I was rather thrilled to receive a letter from someone who had preached in my church. He wrote, "We occasionally remember you in our prayers." I don't

17

know what your reaction would have been to receiving that. "Well, why can't he remember me frequently? And why doesn't he say what other people say — 'I pray for you daily, brother'?" Somehow there was something so honest about the word "occasionally" and I thought, "Great! – he prays for me occasionally. Isn't that lovely?" I knew he was being very careful in what he said. So Paul does not say, "I pray for you every day." He says, "Whenever I pray for you." It is an honest kind of relationship. He is not promising things he can't keep up.

He is so thankful. What is he thankful for? Is it for their health, or their friendliness – no, there is something much deeper. Paul lived for one thing. He said, "One thing I do...." What was this one thing? Personal holiness? No, he had tried that as a Pharisee. What was the one thing that made him tick? Could you put it in a sentence? I can: *he lived for the gospel*. That was the very heart of his life. This was the whole of his ambition: to get that gospel as far as he could, to Spain if necessary. He had been called to take the gospel, and this one thing he did. He was going to get that gospel as far as he could.

So why was he thankful to the Philippians? He was thankful that when he preached to them they listened, believed, accepted, supported and shared. Now that is a response that would make any preacher want to shout "Hallelujah!" Not people saying, "Thank you for the nice sermon," but people who have heard it, believed it, agreed on it, are going to spread it, and will support the preacher to take it elsewhere. That gladdens a preacher's heart, because then it really has got in. It has become a partnership and not just a one-way thing. This is the great desire of the preacher. Believe me, it is a hollow reward to have people just say nice things about the sermon and do nothing about them. Nothing gladdens a preacher who is called to preach the word more than to have people listen, accept, agree, spread, and support what he is doing. No wonder Paul said that every time he thought of them and prayed for them, he gave thanks to God. The ambition of every minister ought to be (and in many cases is) not to have a great ministry himself, but to multiply his ministry in others and to see others taking up what he is seeking to do. There are two sorts of minister, I think, in the world: those who see their own ministry as something to be built up and to be supported, and those who see that ministry spreading so that people want to go away and tell somebody else what they have heard and want to spread that as far as possible.

The second mark of Christian prayer is its *emotional content*. Now I know that there are emotions when other people pray, I know when they get into problems there is the emotion of fear, despair – all sorts of things can get in. But the emotional life of Christian prayer is unique. This prayer that Paul outlines here is shot through with feeling. I was brought up on, "Don't trust your feelings; feelings have no part in faith. Feelings shouldn't get inside your Christianity because they are terribly misleading." Then why did God give me feelings at all? Are they a result of sin or did he make me an emotional being as well as an intellectual one?

Christian prayer is not just cerebral, intellectual prayer, nor is it just saying the right things – it has *heart* in it. Somehow, you know as well as I do, when you are in a prayer meeting when someone is praying with a heart in it and there is feeling there. But I do not mean trying to work up feeling. I do not mean trying to get more excited than we did last prayer meeting. Paul starts talking about the emotion that accompanies his prayer. He is telling the church: I feel desperately homesick for you when I pray for you; I yearn for you; I carry you in my heart. It is not, "I carry you in my mind." The word he uses covers the lungs, heart, liver and kidneys. What an extraordinary word to use! It is translated wrongly as "bowels". He uses this word because in Hebrew thinking and language it is those organs that respond when you are having emotions. Isn't that true? If you have got feelings, you might say, "I love you with all my heart." The heart pumps blood around the body. Why do we say "heart"? That is where you get the sensation of feeling. Paul is yearning for the believers even as his mind is praying for them. Of course there are times when you don't have feelings in your prayer. There are times, in fact, when you feel pretty cold, as if you are talking into a telephone but not getting through.

By nature Paul was not an emotional man, so how was he able to call God to witness about his feelings for them (and only God knows what real feelings there are inside)? The answer is that he is letting them know that Christ has taken over his kidneys, liver, heart and so on. I live, yet no longer I, but Christ lives in me – so when I pray for you I feel what Christ feels for you. That is what makes Christian prayer, so that you can pray for someone and feel what Christ feels.

I share a very intimate thing with you, and I hope you can interpret it rightly. Someone once said to me: "I've been praying for you, and every time I pray I weep for you." It wasn't the person weeping, because they had not intended to weep when they prayed for me. It was Christ taking over. Likewise, when you think of people who are hearing and accepting, supporting, and spreading the gospel, there is a joy deep down. You think: that's great; isn't that exciting? Isn't that encouraging? Oh, I'm so thrilled. That is the second note I wanted to mention.

The third and last note in this prayer is a rather deeper one that will stretch your mind. Christian prayer is always set in a time scale. One of the unique features of the Bible which distinguishes it from every other book in any other religion is that it is right inside the time line of history, and history is *his* story, and the Bible is a book of history. God is the God who is and who was and who is to come; God is the God of the past, present, future, and Jesus is yesterday, today and forever. What difference does that make to your prayer? Natural prayer is existential, and if that word means nothing to you let me explain it. Natural prayer is only concerned with the present. It is saying, "Lord, this is where I am, this is my need. Help! I need help!" It is just a prayer from the present up to heaven. The old Greek idea of time was that time goes in a circle, history repeats itself, it doesn't get anywhere – there is no progress and no purpose, so when you pray, you pray to eternity, which is outside of time, it is a kind of cloud above the circle. That was the Greek idea of time but the Hebrew idea of time is a line from the past through the present to the future, and it is a one-way line. God is bound up with time. I am not going to say God is *in* time, I am going to say time is in God. That is the Hebrew concept, and therefore eternity is not a cloud above all this. Eternity is from everlasting to everlasting, it is time extended forever. Christian prayer is not getting out of this circle of time up into the cloudy eternity. Christian prayer is from the past, through the present, to the future. Before considering what to pray in the present, it asks, "Where has God brought us from, where is he taking us to – and in the light of that, what is our need now?" What a difference! So how does Paul pray for the Philippians? He says first of all: "I think of the good work that God began in you from the very first day." It was God who started it off, so Paul is saying: Think of the beginning, from the very first day God began it, and I am confident that the God who began it is going to complete it in the day of Jesus Christ. Paul is not concerned with their present need in itself. He is concerned with the present only in so far as it is moving from the past to the future. He has such confidence that God who began will complete it.

I have that confidence. Some people get afraid that things might go terribly wrong, that there might be disaster. God never begins something that he won't see through. It is in that confidence that you can pray for the next bit of his work in the life of those about whom you are thinking. Paul wrote, "I know that God began a good work," and he was not thinking of individuals, he was thinking of the church at Philippi. He knew that God who began that work was going to complete it, so he knew what to pray for.

That is how we too can pray for a church. Not, "Lord, leave us be, let us settle down here. Lord, let's stay as we are for a bit, please." No, pray that you may press on, forgetting the things that are behind and stretching forward. There it is again in Philippians 3 – leaving that and heading on for this; on the move. That is because God is always on the move. He walks – have you noticed that? I know sometimes we want to run, but the temptation I think is more often to sit!

That, then, is the past: God who *began* a good work in you. That is also the future. Paul is absolutely convinced that God will complete it. But this does not mean he just sits back to watch him. He prays the next bit of the work in. Now we come to the crucial point. What is it that Paul is praying for them as the next little move – the next step forward?

I am afraid there is a comma in at least one version which I wish wasn't there. It is not there in the original. Paul does not pray: "That your love may abound more and more." That is too easy a prayer. That is too vague and general a prayer, like "Lord, give us more" to which I am sure the Lord would say: What do you mean by that? How do you expect to see that answered? Paul prays that *your love may abound more and more in knowledge and discernment* – in other words, that you may have a particular kind of love. This word "love" is misleading. Paul wants *real* love for his people: that your love may have in it knowledge and discernment. Real love is not based on ignorance or blindness. Love is prepared to know. A large congregation is not a situation in which you can learn love. How can you when you can't possibly have knowledge of each other? A big church needs to be committed to smaller groups where we can know people by name, know their weaknesses and strengths, and love what we know. Real love, genuine love. "Let your love be genuine, hold fast to what is good and abhor what is evil." You can't do that until you know someone well enough to know what is good and what is wrong, and to deal with both in love. That is love with knowledge and discernment. Discernment means not only to know about the person, but to be able to see what needs encouraging and what needs rebuking. Large congregations cannot abound in love in knowledge and discernment. There is a place for large congregations, a place for celebration and for worship, but even if we can talk about it and sing about it in large numbers meeting together, we cannot abound in knowledge and discernment in such a setting.

Why does Paul pray for this? There are four purposes. First: that you may choose what is best. Real love makes constant choices. Think of Jesus facing death and he drops in at a home where he has always been so welcome, where there is ready hospitality, a home that I suppose was the nearest thing he had during his three years' ministry to a home of his own – a home in Bethany. Martha invites him to sit down while she goes into the kitchen to cook. She is not doing anything wrong. It is a good thing to want to give somebody a good meal. But Mary chose what was best. She knew him and discerned that he wanted somebody to talk to. Isn't that lovely? That's the kind of love that Paul longs for, so that you know people well enough to know what they need, so that you can discern, perhaps so that you can send them an understanding letter. So you can say the right word to them. Approving what is excellent or choosing what is best is one of the marks of growing in maturity. When you are a young Christian you have to learn to choose between the bad and the good. When you have learned to do that, the next lesson is to choose between what is good and what is better. The final lesson is to choose between what is better and best. The mark of maturity, growing up, is that a person does not fill his life with good things, but chooses what is best. One can easily fill one's diary with what is good and miss what is best. O God, give knowledge and discernment to approve what is excellent.

This may be about choosing what it is best to do on a Sunday. A lady once asked me, "What can I do about my husband? I've been a Christian for six months, as you know, and it is wonderful, but he is getting further and further away from me and he's not interested. I've told him about the gospel, I've told him he's a sinner, I told him he needs the Saviour, I've told him what wonderful sermons we get, I've told him he ought to come along and hear, and he's just not responding. What should I do?"

I answered, "You should stop coming to church twice a Sunday and you should spend the rest of Sunday with your husband."

"Oh well, he just watches television."

"Watch it with him. That is the excellent thing, the better thing."

She was a bit cross and said, "But I'm hungry for the word and I'm growing, I need to learn so much and I'm responding and I love it. Isn't that a good thing?"

I replied, "It's not the best. You go home."

So she went home and the next Sunday there he was, watching the television, "Aren't you going to church?"

"No."

"Why not?"

"Well, I want to be with you."

"What for?"

After a bit, do you know the result? Within weeks he was sitting in church with her because she had chosen the *best* thing. Her love was getting a bit of knowledge and discernment.

A Christian fellowship needs to choose what is best. You can't do everything you want in church, and you certainly can't in life. Sooner or later you discover that life is too short, and many people get into their fifties and look back and say, "Well, I've had a good life, I've had a good career, we've had a good family, but I somehow feel I've missed the best." They have missed the best because of a choice – not between good and bad, but a choice between good and best. Paul means: I want your love to abound in knowledge and discernment so that you may approve what is excellent and choose the very best thing to do, the very best thing for the fellowship, the very best thing for you.

It may be that instead of rushing away to do some catering you go and sit at Jesus' feet for a bit. That might be the best thing, or whatever your equivalent is of filling your life with good things. That is the first purpose.

Here is the second: from that, you may be pure and blameless. The word "pure" there is a lovely word. It means "transparent" so that people can see right through you. Paul wants see-through saints, and that we may be blameless. This means: so that in the day of Christ he can never say to you, "You filled your life with so many good things that you missed the best." Then Paul moves on in the purpose: *That you may therefore produce the fruits of righteousness that those things that only Christ can produce in you will appear.*

That is still not the final purpose. I want you to abound in love, in the love that has knowledge and discernment, in order to choose what is best, in order to be pure and blameless, in order to produce the fruits of righteousness, in order to—what? What is the final one in the chain of purposes? *In order that you may bring praise and glory to God through Christ Jesus*—that is what it is all about. So people can look at you and say, "Praise God!" So that people can look at you not just as an individual but as a fellowship, and say, "What a wonderful God they must have." It was said of two famous preachers in London that when you heard one you went away saying, "What a great preacher he is," and when you heard the other you went away saying, "What a great Saviour Jesus is." That is what it is all about: that you may be to the praise and the glory of his name.

What is the secret of taking such an ordinary thing as addressing a letter and transforming it in such a way? Look at the word that occurs most often, namely *Christ*. From Paul and Timothy, servants of *Christ*, to the saints in Philippi in *Christ*, grace and peace to you from *Christ*, I yearn for you with the affection of *Christ*, to the glory of God in *Christ*.

Please read Philippians 1:12–26

Wherever God is moving, wherever there is a work going forward, wherever there is progress to denigrate, the vested interest of Satan, the father of lies, is in criticising it and starting rumours, libels, slander. The enemy is a master at this tactic and we are not unaware of his devices. But he cannot do it unless there are people who have wrong feelings, who enjoy being the first with bad news and get a kick out of passing on gossip – unless there are people who actually respond to Satan's desire to plant this kind of thing. The way to combat this is information. The truth is always the thing that the devil fears most. He likes a half-truth and he likes a lie, but he cannot stand the truth. Therefore it is very important that in Christian circles the truth be passed on as quickly and clearly as possible, and that kills the kind of false rumours which the devil loves to plant. This is why Paul wants the Philippians to *know* – to have an accurate account of where he is, what the pressures are, what his real situation is. He did not want believers to listen to rumours.

I get many prayer letters from various people in Christian service. Most of them I never asked for, but nevertheless they come through my letter box with unfailing regularity. I find it very interesting reading them because they differ so much. Some prayer letters are just a list of engagements and things that have been done, places visited, numbers attending and so on. All facts, but they don't give me anything of the feelings of the person writing. They don't bare their heart;

they don't tell me they are feeling homesick. They don't tell me what's going on inside.

Paul, writing to the Philippians, gives us a model prayer letter. It is not just a list of things he is doing, certainly not a list of places where he has been, because he can't go anywhere. But he opens the doors of his heart and lets us right in, so much so that at one point his language becomes disjointed, he is agitated, in tension – in such stress that the commentators are almost in despair as they try to put his grammar together. There is strong feeling coming out and he lets his readers see what the tension is so that they can pray properly.

In fact, many of the things that they are already praying for are quite wrong and they don't need to pray about them. He has heard from Epaphroditus that they are very anxious about him. They are worried about him being depressed and about him facing possible death. So we might think of them praying for him that the Lord would keep Paul's spirits up, keep him from being too depressed and frustrated by being chained up. But he could let them know that was not the situation at all. They did not need to pray about that. He was raring to go, longing to depart. We can be praying for the wrong things, given a lack of information about people's real feelings.

He wanted the brethren to know that the effect of the things that had happened to him was not what you would have expected but the exact opposite. He had really been through it for five years – going right back to the day in Jerusalem when he was nearly lynched by a mob in the temple, saved from that by the temple guard, given a rough kind of trial, hearing of a plot to assassinate him in prison, escorted by soldiers and cavalry down to Caesarea, put in prison for two years, given at least two hearings where his innocence is declared, yet still left in prison. Finally he had been packed off to Rome in a boat, free of charge, but having to cope with a shipwreck halfway, and then arriving in Rome.

I will never forget the day, one Easter Sunday morning, when I walked along the Appian Way on the very stones on which Paul walked. I tried to imagine what he would have been thinking as he walked up this road chained between two Roman soldiers. He came over that hill and saw ahead the magnificent metropolis of Rome. Here was this little man coming to the most mighty city the then known world had seen. I thought of those words: "I'm not ashamed of the gospel. It is the power of God to salvation to everyone who believes." Paul was coming to the head of an empire that worshipped military might, power. Roman might had established Roman law, custom, everywhere in the then known world, and here he was with the gospel in his heart, walking into that city a prisoner. Yet he had within him the power which would convert even the Roman emperor not many centuries later.

Did the Philippians think that the things which had happened to Paul had become a pressure? Were they thinking that his couple of years in Rome chained to a Roman soldier, confined to one house, were getting him down? Did they think he was cracking up, getting depressed? If so, they were absolutely wrong. He could assure them that it was the best thing that could have happened to him.

So let us look first at the things he is not concerned about and then at the things he is concerned with. That is what a prayer letter should do. It should correct those who are praying, so that they know what the real pressures are.

First, he is not worried about what has happened to him in the past. It is not a pressure on him. It is not a load, because it has helped and not hindered. He uses a Greek word which means literally removing road blocks to a traveller. What had happened to him had removed the road blocks. Far from being a blockage to what his ambition was, it has removed the blocks and he had been able to get through to where he wanted to be. It had helped him in doing what he wanted to do, so they need not be worried about what had happened to him in the past.

Nor was he worried about what might happen to him in the future. He might face having his head chopped off but that was not a pressure to him, not a burden. He was not anxious about it, so they did not need to pray about it. These would be two things that might have been prayed about.

Many years ago, some believers in Nepal were arrested and thrown in prison. Some of them were from a fellowship in India. When the news got back to India a prayer meeting gathered and they began to say, "Lord, keep them safe," "Lord, get them out of prison," and round the circle these prayers went, until the turn came to an Indian woman who lifted up her face in joy and said, "Lord, why did you give them the privilege of suffering for you and not us?" The whole atmosphere of the prayer meeting changed. If you just pray for what you think is the human need, you might be right off course. Paul might be in chains, but he was not doubting and he was not in the grip of despair.

We have heard so much teaching on getting your way out of awkward circumstances through praise: "When you are weighed down under a load of circumstances, when everything is going wrong, then keep on saying, 'Hallelujah, praise the Lord' until you have popped up again." Have you heard this? Now the impression you could get from this letter is that he has had an almighty battle over very trying circumstances but has just kept saying, "Hallelujah, praise the Lord," until he has come out on top of them and is now able to say, "I've got the victory, I'm over my circumstances." I remember asking someone, "How are you?" to which he replied: "Over the circumstances, very well." That is one concept of victory in the Lord. But Paul here is *not* rejoicing because he has conquered the circumstances. He is rejoicing because the circumstances are good. He is assuring his readers that it has worked out great. Everything that had happened to him had been for the progress of the gospel, and that is what he lived for. His ambition was fulfilled, his dreams were coming true. He was not frustrated but fulfilled.

How could that be? Well, you have to get your ambitions right to be able to do that. Had Paul had the wrong ambitions then he would have been trying to praise *under* the circumstances, he would have been fighting this, he would have been praying, "Lord, give me grace to bear this, give me victory over it." But because his ambition was the gospel and because these circumstances were furthering the gospel, he had no problem in praising the Lord.

What was his ambition? Paul the great strategist, Paul the master missionary had the ambition to plant the gospel in every key centre, so that from there it could spread out. His sights were set on the very limits of the known world. He wanted even to get to Spain if he could, not for a holiday on the Costa del Sol but to go and plant the gospel in some strategic place. But his biggest ambition of all was to get to Rome. That is where it all happens. Anything that gets established in Rome will spread out along those Roman roads to the whole world.

There was a church there before Paul arrived, so he is busy writing to it. It is the only church he ever wrote to before he had founded it. He wrote them a letter and said: I'm coming to see you. I just want to help you there; I want to make you strong. I want to impart a spiritual gift to you. His ambition was to help to make a really strong Christian presence in the capital. His arrest in Rome, his imprisonment in Caesarea, his voyage – everything had led to the fulfilment of his highest dreams. The gospel was now being planted in Rome. So he was not a man who had praised himself through to victory. Here was a man who saw that God is sovereign and that every circumstance is furthering the gospel, not hindering it – removing the roadblocks, not establishing them; getting Paul to his destination, so he is happy to say that he can rejoice. His coming in chains meant he got the gospel right into the imperial palace. Wasn't that exciting? If he had come as a free preacher they would probably have paid no attention to him. Walking past the household cavalry barracks in London, I thought, "If you got Paul in there as a prisoner, you could really get right into the centre of things." That is exactly what happened. The "household cavalry" of those days was the Praetorian Guard. Nine thousand men, the elite of the Roman army carefully picked, on double pay, were the only soldiers who got a pension. They lived next to the imperial palace. They were the elite soldiers of an empire in which military might was a god.

The Lord had put Paul right there and the whole place was talking about him. No wonder! They had never had a prisoner like that. For one thing, he had not committed a crime. He had not rebelled against Rome. He had not broken Roman law. He was a Roman citizen. They would ask, "What are you in for then?" He could answer, "I am just in because I believe that God sent his Son to this world."

"They put you in prison for that?"

People knew that he was a prisoner because of his believing in Christ and that there was something different about him.

I would not give anything for the chances of an atheist or an agnostic who is chained to Paul for eight hours a day! The soldiers would take turns. They probably had a rota to keep away from him! But sooner or later they would find themselves chained to him, and to be chained to Paul would be to be chained to Jesus Christ. Can you imagine being chained to Christ for eight hours a day? Think of what they would hear. They would hear Paul praying. They would hear him speaking in tongues, because he did that more than anybody at Corinth, so he was doing it quite a lot. But it indicates that he did it in private. You don't pray in silence when you pray in tongues, so they must have been pretty astonished at the number of languages this prisoner knew. They were exposed to his prayer life and to his preaching. They were exposed to his correspondence, "Take a letter for the saints at Philippi, please" – and he would dictate it and they had to listen to all that. "Strange letter – he's happy to be here in prison. He's thrilled to bits that he is chained to a Roman soldier!" Can you see the word spreading so quickly? What wouldn't we give to have nine thousand of the top men in the forces in Britain – Royal Air Force, Navy, and Army – chained to Christians for eight hours at a time? Mind you, what an acid test for Christians! Would you like to be chained to an unbeliever every moment of your life, so they see everything you do, every reaction you have? What a test!

Paul not only says that the whole Praetorian Guard are listening now, but all the others too. Who does he mean? He would be meeting lawyers and speaking to magistrates and court officials as they prepared his case. All that was an open door into the very heart of the Roman Empire – what a door for the gospel.

Then the second thing that had happened as the result of his imprisonment was that the local Christians in Rome, far from being depressed by his imprisonment, were saying: now that Paul is in prison we really must take up the burden; let's preach the gospel. They were filled with courage because he was showing such courage. Think of a high profile Christian being arrested by the police in your locality, and that you were able to go and see him, and every time you did he was praising God that things were working out so well, and that all the police in the police station were listening now. What effect would that have on you? I think you would be wanting to talk about Jesus too, wouldn't you? Paul was thrilled, as any minister would be, not by having a lot of people listen to him, but people listening in such a way that they became preachers – and that they passed on the message. The whole church in Rome was excited and emboldened.

Paul's ambition was to give them some spiritual gift. Have you ever asked what gift he wanted to impart to them? He may not have known, but I know which one they needed and which he gave them. It was the first or second gift of the Spirit on the day of Pentecost and in the early chapters of Acts. It was the gift of *a holy boldness in speaking*. If you study Acts, again and again you see that the Holy Spirit came on them and they spoke the Word of God with *boldness*, a forthrightness, an openness of speech. This was the spiritual gift that Paul was going to give the church in Rome. They probably had all the others anyway. Because he came in chains and because he was in prison and because he had such courage and such joy in prison, this imparted the spiritual gift of boldness to the people. So they were fearlessly proclaiming the message of God and nothing could thrill Paul more.

I dare to associate with that. I could cope with being shut up myself if the result would be that others were out speaking and preaching the gospel, because that would be much more exciting than doing it myself. That was Paul's response to this situation.

Then he mentions a rather sad fact. Christians can get their motives mixed up, and even their speaking can be motivated wrongly. One of the effects that Paul's visit to Rome had was this: when he came to Rome it seemed as if he was suddenly the focus of the whole church, and it rather put out those who were the teachers and preachers there already. They were a little fed up that everybody was talking about the great apostle Paul who was now in Rome. They had their noses pushed out a bit. The result was that envy and jealousy, party feeling, came in. So when he was incarcerated and chained up, some of them said: now we can be the preachers, we can get our status back, we can get our position. So they preached really hard, not only to take Paul's place because they were jealous of him, but they even had the malicious motive in their heart that they thought it would really get him irritated to hear that they were more successful while he was shut up.

Paul knew they were doing it from wrong motives. He knew they were jealous of him. "I know they want to make my chains irritate me even more; they want to make me sore." But it had the exact opposite effect. He did not mind why people went out preaching, as long as they got out preaching Christ.

What a big man this is – what a big heart he has! He is not the slightest bit upset that people are trying to take his place. His attitude is: Hallelujah, may more people take my place! That is his response. It is like water off a duck's back; he doesn't have a battle over it because he is living for the gospel of Christ. If you are living for the gospel, you don't care who is spreading it or even why they are spreading it, as long as they are spreading it. So the Philippians need not pray about that irritation if they hear about it: that people are trying to make his imprisonment painful by stepping into his shoes and taking over while he is in there. Instead they can just rejoice. Hallelujah, Christ is being *placarded*. That is the word he uses: "advertised". Everywhere people are hearing about Christ. Let me make it quite clear that Paul would not approve of those who are getting the *message* wrong. He does not mind what their motives are, but he does mind what the message is. So this is not applicable to the kind of sects that we have problems with. He is not thinking, "Ah well, as long as these people are mentioning Christ, that's okay." What he doesn't mind is if some preach the right message for the wrong motives. It is the message that saves people, not the motives of the person preaching it.

I knew an evangelist called Herbert Silverwood. A delightful former club comedian, he became a preacher. One of his favourite pulpits was the seafront. He took a whole mission cinema van from the Methodist church. What he did was show films out of the back of the van. I worked for a year in one of those vans, so I can sympathise with his task. He would show a film, then preach at the end of it and invite people to respond. He had a man driving the van and running the projector, a good engineer who was not a Christian. One day Herbert was ill with flu and had to stay in bed. So he said to his driver, "Take the day off. Go and enjoy yourself. I'm not going to be on the seafront today."

The driver said, "Well, I have nothing to do. Do you mind if I go and show some films?"

Herbert replied, "Alright, you go and show some films." So he showed some films and got quite a crowd. When he had gone through all the films, there they were still. So this driver, an agnostic, got up and said word for word everything that Herbert Silverwood would have said at the end! Then he came running back to the boarding house where Herbert was staying and said, "I've got two enquirers, what do I do with them? Tell me what to say next!"

You see, it is the message that saves, not the messenger. I can't save a soul, but the message I preach can. Paul says that it is by the foolishness of the preaching that people get saved. It is the "foolishness" not of the messenger but of the message.

So Paul does not care about their motives. Some can do it because they love him and some because they hate him, but as long as they are preaching the message he is happy because of this. That is quite an insight into Paul. There is no self pity there, just a man who believes in the sovereignty of God – who believes that God is on the throne and no satanic agency and no human stubbornness can get God off the throne, and that God will order his circumstances in such a way that his ambitions will be fulfilled and his dreams realised, because those ambitions are the right ones and not the wrong ones. His ambition was to take the gospel of Christ to people, and everything that has happened has helped and not hindered.

So Paul is not trying to persuade himself to praise the Lord in trying circumstances. He is praising him for those circumstances because they are so good. So what should they pray for him in these circumstances, in the light of what has happened to him? He asks just one thing: please pray that I will not fail in my duty; please pray that I will not let the Lord down; please pray especially now. Why especially now? Well, he is coming up to the trial – the time is approaching when he is going to be most on public view in Rome. There will be a lot of curiosity. People will crowd the court to hear this man's case. Paul did not care whether he lived or died.

Daniel Poling, an American, established a worldwide movement. He had a son who went into the forces as a chaplain. Daniel and his wife prayed every day, "Lord, please bring our son safely home again after the war." After a while they realised that they were praying the wrong prayer and they changed. They started praying together by their bed, "Lord, whether our boy comes back or not, may he honour Christ." Their son was on a ship that was torpedoed in the Atlantic. The ship was going down and there were not enough lifebelts for the troops on board. He and two other chaplains took off their lifebelts and gave them to three others. They linked arms – a Jewish chaplain, a Protestant and a Catholic chaplain – and they sang praise to God. The last people saw of them was as they went down on the ship. That incident was commemorated on an American postage stamp which shows the three of them linking arms and singing as they went down. The story went right around America and Christ was honoured, so the prayers were answered and dreams fulfilled because they were the right prayers, the right dreams.

So we can understand that Paul did not want his readers to pray about terrible circumstances – the circumstances were wonderful. There was no need to wonder whether he was getting depressed or cracking up or whether everything was getting on top of him. He was letting them know that everything was great as far as that goes. They were to pray that he might honour Christ and not let him down or fail in his duty.

Now Paul turns to the future and what might happen to him. What could happen? Within a few weeks of writing this letter he could be in his grave. He is probably in his mid-fifties, still with a lot of life in him. But he is facing death. It will be a quick death. As a Roman citizen he is entitled not to be crucified but to be beheaded – a flash of a sword and a second and it is over, so that it would not be a painful death. But it would be death. It has been said that the real test of someone's religion is what it does for him when he comes to die. Another thought is that the task of the Christian preacher is to prepare those in the prime of life for death. Indeed, Christians are unashamed to face people who are in the prime of life with the fact of death, because it raises the most important question. The reason why people are running away from death, why they don't want to talk about it, why it is a taboo subject, is because they don't want to face this question: *what is life all about?* We are like the tourist who jumped into a taxi outside Waterloo Station and said, "Drive on, drive on!" And the driver replied, "Where to?" He said, "I'm in too much of a hurry, drive on!" Death says, "Where are you driving *to*? What's it all about? What are you living for?" Now why should death produce that question? Because death will either come as loss or gain to you, depending on what you are living for. That is why death is such a searching fact and why it poses this question. If you are living for money, then you don't want to hear about death because you are going to lose it. You will leave everything. Even if you are living for people (and that is better than living for things), if you are living for your family, then death poses the question: what will I do to you? What are you living for? Until you have answered that question satisfactorily, death poses a threat. There are only two kinds of people who are ready to die: those who say there is nothing left to live for, and those who say: "To me, to live is Christ, therefore death is gain." Once again we get a wrong impression if we think Paul had a great big battle with the fear of death, a great big battle with the anxiety about it; and that somehow, by forcing himself to praise the Lord, he managed to rise above that. Far from it! He is looking forward to it. The facts are right and his feelings are just following the facts. He is not trying to bolster his feelings against the facts. The facts are that he is possibly going to die in the next few weeks and he can say "Hallelujah!" He is not saying that to lift himself but because it is absolutely true. He is going to be far better off. If to live is Christ, then to die is more Christ. I challenge you to ask yourself: are you living for your family before you live for Christ? If so, then death will come as a threat. Death will ask you where your priorities lie.

What would be your first reaction if you were told now, "You will not be in church next Sunday because you are going to die before then? If you are living for Christ your first reaction would be, "Hallelujah, next Sunday I'm with Jesus" and your second reaction would be, "But what about my family?" But if you are living for your family first, your first reaction would be, "What will happen to my family?" Then your second reaction might be, "But never mind – I'll be with Christ." Which would be your first reaction?

For Paul, to live is Christ. People say, "Ah, but Paul was a bachelor, he didn't have the kind of ties and links that other people had." Don't you believe it – Paul had a very big family. If you could have said to Paul, "You're not a family man. You didn't have those close ties with people, those emotions to understand that we can't just say, 'Oh, it'd be lovely to go and be with Christ'" Paul would have answered, "I have a big family and I am torn. But I know who comes first – for me to live is Christ, and to die is gain."

I have heard so many examples of this kind of attitude to death. Once I was talking to an elderly retired deaconess in London. I had not seen her for some fifteen years. She was radiant as she always was. I said, "How are you?"

"I'm longing to go, but the Lord keeps me down here for some reason." That was her immediate reaction. You could see it in her face.

I think of a man in Buckinghamshire who called all his relatives to come and stay when he knew he was dying. He said, "Come and see how a Christian dies."

I think of George Tomlinson, a former Minister of Education who was visited in his very serious illness by a minister who asked, "What are your prospects?" He replied, "They're good! If I get better I'm going to Blackpool and rest there with my wife, and if I don't I'm going to heaven and rest with my Saviour." Such is the genuine mark of someone who is living for the right things.

Paul is telling them that they do not need to worry about

his dying. This is the point at which his language becomes agitated, his grammar goes haywire and the verbs and the nouns chase each other over the page. Clearly he is getting very tense, but he is in a terrible dilemma. He is worried that he might have to go on living. He wanted to be off, to depart, and the word he uses for "depart" is delightful – it is the word for pulling up your tent pegs, and Paul was a tent maker. He was ready to pull up his tent pegs! But then he lets the Philippian believers know he is thinking about them, his family. He thinks about all those who need him, his children in the Lord. He really did not know which to choose.

When I read about that, I almost want to say to Paul, "Do you think it's your choice then?" In fact it was, because when he went to the trial he could either put up a good defence and get himself off or he could just let them walk over him. So he did have a choice in a sense and Paul is saying he is torn between the two. He had been praying: he wanted to be with the Lord, but knew that his children needed him – what did the Lord think? The Lord wanted him to stay a bit. Paul's face must have dropped. You mean I can't come to be with you? Not just yet, Paul, they need you.

So Paul knew that he was going to be released. He had that witness in him, a strong conviction the Lord was going to let him remain for a while for their sake, not for his – he did not want to. But for the Lord, he would stay. What did they need from him? He is burdened for two things, like any church leader: a burden for their *progress* and their *joy*. There is a connection there. One of the first reasons for losing your joy is that you have stopped making progress. There is no standing still in the Christian life. If you try to, if you say, "No more changes, no more progress, no more moving," then you will lose your joy, because the joy is in the travelling and the joy of knowing that you haven't arrived and the joy of doing new things every day with Jesus. That is where the joy comes from: making progress in the faith, moving, knowing I am not the same as I was last week or last month or last year. That is why, in Psalm 51, David, who had come to a spiritual standstill, says, "Restore to me the joy of my salvation...." I have stopped and I have slipped back, get me going again.

Paul knows that he should remain so that they may make progress and get their joy back. So as far as his future goes, he is going to ask them to pray for his release, convinced that with their prayers and God's supply of the Spirit, he would be set free.

So he does ask them to get him out of prison through prayer, as Peter was got out of prison through prayer. But notice that he is not asking them to do it for his own comfort or his own safety. He is saying: Pray for my release for your sake and, when I come to you, you will have even more to be exalting Christ about.

That is his prayer letter. Isn't it exciting? I try to imagine what the next church prayer meeting would be like just after Philippi had received this prayer letter – and what the last one had been like. I imagine a complete transformation of the meeting. I can see them at Philippi before they got the letter saying: Lord, Paul is about to die, please get him off! Please keep him safe! Lord, even at this late hour, change the judge's mind and help them to realise he is innocent. And Lord, please keep Paul from getting too depressed and please keep him from getting frustrated....

I can just imagine all that, and then, when they get the letter.... Thursday, the prayer meeting day, and up they come. The Philippian jailer gets up and starts praying first. He says, "Lord, Paul's at it again, I remember him in this prison here and he was singing and I got converted, and now he's converting all the Praetorian Guard – Hallelujah!" There's a complete change in the prayer meeting and it is: "Lord, isn't it exciting to die; isn't it marvellous? Lord, we're going to be a bit selfish, please keep him here a while for us." What a different kind of a prayer meeting! They have realised the *real* needs.

Of course, the biggest concern Paul has in prison is not about what has happened to him or what could happen to him – it is for the Philippians, that whether he is able to come and see them or whether he is absent, he may hear that they are standing fast in one Spirit and fighting together for the gospel of Christ.

Please read Philippians 1:27–30

Paul's letter to the Philippians is a letter from an apostle to a church and that is one key that unlocks the meaning. Secondly, it is a letter from a very Jewish Jew to Gentile believers. That is another key that unlocks its meaning. But there is a third key, and perhaps one of the most important to our understanding of this letter: it comes from a Roman citizen to a Roman colony.

I was brought up to think about Rome, partly because every day when I went to school I walked or cycled past a wall about sixty feet in length. It was part of the remains of the Roman wall that stretched right across the country from Carlisle to the River Tyne. Then, when I had a Saturday free I could get on my bike and go off to a place where the Roman wall appears in all its glory as it climbs over the Northumbrian crags. There you can see the Roman camps, perfectly excavated, and study the life that went on inside them and the methods of defence. You could see the baths. You could see the houses, the central heating. You could go into the museum and study the remains of clothes, jewellery and weapons – all kinds of things that belonged to the Roman way of life.

Imagine my astonishment when I first had the privilege of climbing Masada in Israel, that fortress on the edge of the Dead Sea, and from the top looking down and getting the strange feeling that I had been there before. There was the Roman wall, there were the square fortresses. There inside were exactly the same shaped ruins I had seen as a boy near my home in Newcastle. This was the other end of the Roman Empire from Hadrian's Wall in the North of England, yet it was the same way of life, the same style of defence, the same architecture, the same weapons, the same baths, the same theatres – everything we associate with that empire. That culture implanted in every part of the known world a way of life that was quite distinct.

On the back of the Roman Empire went the Christian colonists. Indeed, the Roman Empire and the Christian church grew simultaneously. It was because Roman colonies had been established everywhere, with a Roman way of life, and Roman roads and all sorts of other Roman customs, that Paul was able as a Roman citizen to travel from one place to another and establish colonies for Christ.

Somehow empire building and missionary work have nearly always gone hand in hand. That may be a good or a bad thing depending on your viewpoint, but one of the reasons that missionary interest in England has declined is precisely that the British Empire declined. The concept of having something to give other countries – and the concept of going elsewhere to establish a way of life – has died, both for the British Empire and for church thinking. This may be why the vast majority of missionaries today come from North America. As Americans have been establishing the American way of life all over the world, so on the back of that imperial influence has gone Christian missionary work. Church history tells a similar story elsewhere, such as with the conquests of Latin America by Spain and Portugal. Wherever an earthly empire was being established, Christians could ride in on the top of that and establish colonies for Jesus Christ. That is what Paul was doing. When he wrote as a Roman citizen to a Roman colony in Philippi he was using language, thought forms, pictures, ideas which belonged to a colonising empire. Colonising is very much frowned upon today. The attempt to take one way of life and plant it in another country is regarded as out of date. But Christians are committed to colonising for Jesus Christ; they are committed to building an "empire". We are imperialists in the deepest sense of the word. Our task is to establish colonies of Christ with a lifestyle that belongs to heaven wherever we can, and we make no apology for that kind of colonising.

Paul planted a colony of heaven in Philippi because that was a key place for a colony. That is why the Romans went there. Paul planted a colony for Christ within the Roman colony in Greece. His fears for the colony are exactly the same as the fears for any colony, as we shall see.

Whenever there is a colony planted, there are two things that can happen which can destroy it. Those two dangers are implicit in these verses. One is an internal danger: that the colony can crack up from the inside. The other is an external danger: that it can be attacked from the outside and destroyed.

Let us think about a Roman colony. It was a group of people, a community who lived entirely as if they were in the metropolis of Rome itself. Their dress, their food, their sport, their leisure activities, their law courts, their justice – every single part of their life was identical with the life of those who lived in the capital itself. That is what made it a colony. It was a metropolis in miniature. Once you got into one of these colonies it felt no different from being back home.

The second thing that kept it a colony was that there would be a ring of crack troops, soldiers who were noted for their courage, their bravery – their ability to stand against overwhelming odds without fear. If you have ever seen pictures of Romans making a stand against a large alien army you will see a picture of what kept the colonies going. So a colony was constituted by its character and its defences – its citizens living the way Roman citizens did, and its soldiers fighting courageously to preserve that little colony. The result was that these colonies, established all over Europe and North Africa, were able to hold the empire.

Now those are the two things, and two dangers were related to them. The first was that the Roman citizens "went native", a phrase which was well understood in the days of the British Empire. Some district officer away in the jungles of Africa who had afternoon tea with brown bread and butter and then dressed for dinner was doing that quite deliberately to preserve the British way of life in the middle of the jungle. If he went native and stopped dressing for dinner, and if he stopped hoisting the Union flag at sunrise and lowering it at sunset, if he took in a native woman, if he started drinking himself silly, then the whole thing began to crack. It was vital to the British Empire that British people behaved in a British way wherever they were – keeping their character. In a Roman colony this same thing could happen. Roman citizens who became more attracted to the culture of the country in which they were living began to dress in a different way and eat in a different way and be interested in different kinds of sport, then very quickly that colony became less of an influence for the empire. It became vulnerable, and in that area the Roman hand would have to be withdrawn.

The other thing that could happen would be that morale amongst the soldiers slipped. When it did, instead of a few Roman soldiers with their shields and spears lining up shoulder to shoulder, closed ranks, putting those spears as a solid barrier to the enemy, they panicked and ran, and then of course the colony was overrun. These are the two dangers in every Christian colony too. The one is a matter of character, the other a matter of defence.

Paul's concern here is not about himself, but about the church. They were a colony of heaven, and he was concerned firstly that they were not compromised inside regarding their way of life. Secondly, that when they faced the enemy together they would not be intimidated or frightened, that they would not panic – not running but holding firm. Then they would not lose any ground and their enemies would find in that the token of their own ruin and doom.

If the character of the colony has gone within, it would be much more difficult for the morale of the troops to defend it outside, and these things are really two sides of the same problem. So Paul says, "Only let your way of life be worthy of the gospel." That is the first thing. When you face enemies do not be frightened in anything. Never panic. Never stampede, never run, but stand firm together in one Spirit, shoulder to shoulder in closed ranks like Roman soldiers defending a colony. That is our situation in churches today, whether we realise it or not. We are colonies of heaven.

First, there was the danger of compromise within. Paul is teaching the people that they must keep up the standards whether he is present or not – certainly not leaning on him. If you lean on any human being then your experience is borrowed. There is only one person to lean on, and that is Christ. I know that he often ministers to us through other people, but if any colony of heaven is leaning on a man then their experience is borrowed and they will collapse. Whether the apostle comes to see them or is absent, they are to lean on Christ.

When Paul says he wants his readers to be living a life that is worthy of the gospel of Christ he means there is to be no compromise within, that there is consistency between what they talk about and how they live. It is very important in a colony of heaven that you are living as heaven is living – as if you were already there, even though you might be a long way off. Roman colonists lived in a particular way even if they never visited Rome during their lifetime.

One of the most startling things Jesus said about it himself was: "No man has ascended into heaven but he who came down from heaven, even the Son of Man who is in heaven." Did you ever notice that last phrase? In other words, for thirty-three years Jesus lived in heaven on earth. He was a little colony of heaven himself, and if you want to know what life in heaven is like, look at Jesus and see. It is an amazing thought. A colony of heaven on earth should so live that people can say, "If you want to know what heaven is like, go and live with those people." What a challenge and what a thought – if you really want to see what the metropolis is like, what the new Jerusalem is like, what the heavenly city is like, then just go to one of its colonies and see how they live.

As we think of "living a life worthy of the gospel" let us look at three dimensions of the gospel. First of all, it is the gospel of *liberty*. It is good news about freedom. It is saying: you are now free, redeemed, you no longer need to live in slavery. Then how do you live a life worthy of the gospel? You live a life worthy of the gospel by not falling into any kind of slavery. If there is a colony of heaven that has fallen into bondage of any kind, it is no longer demonstrating the life of heaven. The gospel of liberty demands that every colony of the gospel is living as a free people. That means avoiding two forms of slavery. There is the form of slavery that is legalism, bringing you into bondage to rules and regulations. Another form of bondage is licence, which brings you into slavery to self and to sin. You have been set free from both. Christ redeemed us from the law, he redeemed us from sin. Therefore, a colony of heaven is a place of free men and women who are living in the liberty of the Spirit, under neither kind of bondage. Christ, who set us free from both bondages, would say: Now live free; the truth sets you free.

That is one example of how a church can fall out of a life

worthy of the gospel: either into legalism or licence, both of
which are common. Funnily enough, those two things which
are opposites are so close together that if you fall into one
it is not long before the other appears. If a church goes into
licence it is not long before there is a legalism trying to stamp
out the licence. If it goes into legalism then people will react
against that legalism into licence. Neither is liberty. We are
preaching a gospel of freedom and a colony of heaven is free.

Another aspect of a colony of heaven is this: the gospel
is the gospel of *life* so a life worthy of the gospel is full of
life. Yet if you go into a church and it feels dead, dreary and
boring, and the minister gets up and says, "We offer abundant
life in the name of Christ," no wonder people say, "Well, if
that's abundant life, I'd rather be dead!" If we are going to
live a life that is worthy of the gospel then it will be a life
that really is life – both abundant and eternal. That means a
colony of people who are excited at the possibility of death,
those to whom death is no threat, those who rejoice at the
saints already in glory who belong to their fellowship and
are looking forward to joining them.

Or take another dimension of the gospel. The gospel we
preach is a gospel of *love*. How then can you have a colony
of heaven in which people are not forgiving one another,
are critical of one another, backbiting and gossiping? The
whole thing just doesn't make sense. It is not a colony of the
gospel. I could give you example after example. There is no
point in a preacher preaching anything if the colony is not
living that way, if people are not saying, "That's the life we
want to live", just as people wanted to be Roman citizens.

There are three notes sounded here where Paul says, "I
want you to live a life worthy of the gospel." There is the
note of *obligation*. If you are going to have the privileges
of the gospel then the responsibilities come with it. The
privilege is that you have been forgiven and promised a place

in heaven. The responsibility is that you live as a citizen of heaven. There is an obligation here to live worthy of the gospel. There is also the thought of a *demonstration*. How is the world going to believe if they only hear but don't see? The world believes what it sees rather than what it hears. The world is looking to see the alternative society. The world is watching this community called Christians and saints. Do we see there the alternative life? Do we see there the good news lived out? When they do, then the church's appeal is irresistible because there is a third note here. Not only is there an obligation to live worthy of the gospel, not only will it be a demonstration, but it will be an *attraction*.

Paul is concerned that just as people's main ambition in the Roman Empire was to become a Roman citizen and get into one of those colonies, so the world should see a church that is saying "This is the life", and the people should want it. Paul, writing to Titus, pleads with him that he should "adorn the doctrine". The word "adorn" there means "put it in nice clothes". A Christian is concerned about the clothes of the doctrine, and the clothes are some things that should be put off and some things put on. There is something much deeper than the clothes you put on your body – it is the clothes you put on the doctrine of Christ. The doctrine is what we preach. The clothes we put on it are how we behave. Paul is saying he wants the world to be attracted to this colony. He wants people to say, "Can we get citizenship, can we get into this kingdom? Could we be part of this great empire?"

Before we leave the phrase "a way of life worthy of the gospel" we note that in fact the way of life is not primarily an individual thing. A Roman colony was not made up of a group of individuals all of whom wore a toga and lay down on a couch to eat their meals. It was made up of a community of people who were Roman in their relationships with each other. Essentially, a colony is a community, not a bunch of individuals. A colony *is* relationships. Therefore when Paul says, "I want your manner of life to be worthy of the gospel", our excessive individualism interprets that nearly always as meaning: "I must live as a Christian should." But Paul is saying he wants believers *together* to demonstrate this, to be the colony.

You cannot be a colony just by attending Sunday services any more than Romans could be a colony by gathering in the stadium to watch the sports. They were a colony in the language they spoke to each other, Latin. They were a colony in the justice they meted out to each other in the courts. They were a colony in everything that they shared together, and when people saw the colony they did not see individuals, they saw a community. Paul is saying: "I want to hear that your manner of life is worthy of the gospel. I want to hear that your living standards, your lifestyle, is the lifestyle of those who are already in heaven, already enjoying eternal life, already living a new lifestyle." So he moves easily on from that thought to their relationships with each other in unity: "I want to hear that you are standing firm in one Spirit, striving together side by side with one mind."

The saddest thing you can ever hear about a church is that they are divided. A colony depends on its unity. As soon as a colony has divided it is wide open to enemy attack. The soldiers who defend it will lose their morale. "What's the point of defending a squabbling group like this?" So Paul's concern that they live a life worthy of the gospel moves naturally into a concern that they remain united, that they stand firm together and that their unity has a common emotion, a feeling for one another, a common ambition, doing the same thing together. Every house, said Jesus, and every city that is divided against itself will fall. There is no quicker way for a church to lose its character as a colony of heaven than to become divided, whatever causes that division or whatever is the ground of it. No wonder that Jesus, on the night in which he was betrayed, on the night before he died, looking at those few men he was leaving behind, a handful, the nucleus of the church, prayed as he did, that they may be one. That meant one in heart, mind and will. If they had been divided, the church would never have got off the ground.

As Jesus was concerned that this little colony of heaven he had established should remain united, so is Paul. The believers are to stand firm, and that expression is the same word used of soldiers in battle, when they are just digging in and they are not going to budge. Having done all, they are going to stand. They had spikes in their shoes to help them to do so. Their feet were shod so, having done all, they could stand very firm right where they were. That is what Paul is anxious about. Unity at the local church level is all important. Nothing damages a church's witness as quickly as division.

Notice that Paul is not interested in a unity without a purpose. It is a unity that is directed to something. It is a unity to a particular objective. You see, churches can be united over different things. You can have a church united over putting up a new building. That is not the unity that Paul would pray for. It certainly is lovely to see people working together and praying together for a new building, but that is not the objective that really holds the colony of heaven together. You can be united in social activities or united in political concerns, but there is only one reason big enough for real unity of a church which is a true colony of heaven, and that is that you are striving and contending together for the faith of the gospel. This above all else, without any distraction, should be your prime concern. That is why we are united, shoulder to shoulder, closing ranks.

Paul clearly means two things when he says that. He

means to *preserve* the gospel and to *propagate* it. One is defensive, one is aggressive. A church that is united for that dual purpose is a church that has found the secret of unity.

In the course of the twentieth century we saw an astonishing preoccupation with unity between churches. There was a never-to-be-forgotten meeting in Lambeth Palace when with representatives around a table of all denominations, from Roman Catholic to Pentecostal, we gathered together and tried to listen to God and felt that God said to us he wanted us to be united, striving together for the faith of the gospel during the 1980s. A new thing happened that day. It was the first time that the leaders of that wide spectrum of UK denominations had come together and decided to strive together, shoulder to shoulder, for that purpose. It was unique.

We felt that an earlier ecumenism which was not so much concerned with the furtherance of the gospel had given way to something more real and deeper. What is needed is a unity that says we must preserve the gospel, we must not allow it to be corrupted, we must not allow heresy to come in. We must hold to the truth that makes us a colony of heaven and the gospel that gives us our character. But we must not only preserve it from getting corrupted, we must propagate it.

Some churches that are only concerned with preserving the gospel become dead. They have a unity that is deadness, they are frozen together. You need the propagation too. But if you propagate without preserving then that will go wrong. Striving together for the faith of the gospel means standing firm for the truth. The word used is the word for horses that see something unexpected and stampede. Paul is saying: I want you in nothing to stampede, in nothing to panic, in nothing to shy. That comes from the Greek word meaning "to go white", to blanch.

We may find ourselves in situations where fear could

take over. The church is changing, excitingly, from being a defensive community to being an aggressive one. There are so many signs of this. I believe God's people in this land are changing from keeping the church going to challenging the world. We are going to be speaking out, stepping out, colonising. We want to take England for King Jesus. That is our mandate and our ambition, and that is going to involve changing people's lifestyle. It is going to involve setting up communities of a new lifestyle all over this land in places where there are no colonies, in key areas.

Part of my work since the 1980s has been going to cities and meeting with Christian leaders, sometimes for a few days, sharing with them, listening to them, helping them to see what God is saying in their situation – how to be a stronger colony and how to colonise. That brings some conflict and controversy. There have been times when there has been real attack. We cannot colonise this land for Christ without opposition. We therefore not only need to be citizens living a life worthy of the gospel, but soldiers who do not panic, who are not afraid, who don't stampede, don't run – who stand firm. "Don't be afraid of your enemies, always be courageous." This proves two things: that they are going to lose and that you are going to win.

Let us look at these two things. First of all, you need to know yourself that you belong to God and that you are going to have the victory. Your enemies also need to know that you are going to win, so that their morale may crumble. Now those two things happen when Christians are unafraid. Time and time again, as you read church history you find that those who persecuted the church became afraid for themselves because the Christians were not afraid. Read *Foxe's Book of Martyrs*.

When you read of what the early Christians went through! They were thrown to the lions and they went marching out into the arena singing hymns to Jesus. Mothers separated from their babies and put in separate cells were told, "You can feed your baby if you'll deny Christ." And they could hear their babies crying in the next cell, but those mothers said, "No, we will not deny Christ." They were unafraid. Roasting them alive on hot spits, their persecutors still could not make them afraid. This lack of fear, this astonishing God-given courage in the first three hundred years of the church, when persecution was at its height, convinced the enemy they had lost and that they were up against God. They knew that they could not prevail.

This was true of Roman colonies. When the enemies, however much they outnumbered the Roman soldiers, saw the Roman defenders stand firm without fear, they knew in their hearts they had lost. It was true of Paul himself. As a young man Paul had stood and held the jackets of the men who had stoned to death Stephen, the first Christian martyr. Stephen died saying, "Father, forgive them! They don't know what they're doing," the same prayer that Jesus had prayed. There was no fear on Stephen's face, and as the stones cut and bruised him and ultimately broke him, he died saying, "Lord Jesus, receive my spirit." There was no fear there.

Paul (or Saul as he was then) knew he had lost. That is why he became a fanatical missionary against Christians. That is why he locked them in prison. That is why he left his own land to go and get some more to persecute, because he knew he had lost and was ruined. He knew that he was heading for destruction. He was kicking against the goads.

If you have read any of Richard Wurmbrand's books you will know that time and time again the communist soldiers torturing Christians came under conviction of sin and fear of God's damnation themselves, because the Christians were not afraid. Time and again they stopped torturing and said, "Tell us about Christ."

It has happened all the way down the line that when a few soldiers of Christ have shown themselves unafraid under attack, the enemy has realised that they have lost the battle. Not only do the enemies realise where they are, but Christians realise where they are too and have confidence. Only if you have been in a situation where you could be mortally afraid, and found that you were not, will you have the assurance that we are thinking of now.

When you read the stories of the ancient church you find this kind of account. As a Roman soldier was putting a Christian to death he mocked him and said, "What is your carpenter doing now?" The reply came, "Making a coffin for your emperor." When you oppose such courage you have lost the battle. Christians get assurance they are going to win.

We find that fear is taken away and God gives the courage. We are not brave people. I am a coward at heart – I run from situations by nature, and perhaps you are not very different. We shall find that God gives us assurance.

A person who is going to lose fights all the harder, desperately, in panic, and Paul's words let his readers know this. The persecutors' panic will show itself in violent attack, but let them panic and let that be an assurance to them of their destruction and to you of your salvation. How do you know that this proves that you are of God? Paul teaches that it is God who grants you to suffer. It is he who not only enabled you to believe in Christ but who gave you the privilege of suffering for him, of getting into the battle. What a different way of looking at it! In *Foxe's Book of Martyrs* and in all the story of Christian suffering down the ages, the one thing you never hear is a Christian saying, "Why should God let this happen to me?" It is extraordinary that I know of no record of those persecutions in which Christians said that. Rather, when suffering came to them in the cause of Christ, this was the note that sounds every time: they rejoice that they were worthy to suffer for the name of Christ. That is an astonishing thing.

Now let me make it plain that the suffering we are thinking about is not the suffering that is the general lot of mankind. A Christian does sometimes ask the question about that kind of suffering – incurable diseases that seem to just pick on saint and sinner alike – and you ask the question, "Why does God let that happen to me?" But when your suffering is due to the fact that you are fighting for Jesus you will not ask that question. When you are in the battle because you are a Christian, because you are colonising for Christ, you will know that God has granted you to suffer for him. You will know that this is your privilege and you will know it because this is the privilege he gave to all his colonisers.

Paul is telling his readers they will be in the same battle as they had seen and heard he was in. They were having the privilege of suffering as he suffered. Jesus said: "Blessed are you when people say all manner of evil against you falsely for my sake because so persecuted they the prophets before you." You are in great company. Martyr after martyr found that when the time came to suffer for Jesus they had been given the privilege of joining the noble army of martyrs.

So Paul is encouraging believers. He doesn't say, "Now you're Christians you can have a nice comfortable time, you can sit in the pew snugly and smugly" or anything like that. He says: "To you God has granted to believe and to suffer."

It had been granted to them to be citizens, to live a life worthy of heaven, but to be soldiers defending that colony against all the attacks that must come. That applies to us too. Why? Because the enemy is the same and Satan does not want England colonised for Christ. Satan does not want the gospel preserved or propagated. Satan does not want these colonies to be established, for he knows that when people see a colony of heaven, deep down they know they have lost, and deep down they know that this is the way and this is the life. So Satan is going to stop that if he can. Paul is telling believers not to be afraid, not to panic – God has granted you this and it is a privilege, a joy and an honour that he should choose you to suffer for him.

I could summarise this by putting it negatively. What Paul does not want to hear from them is that their lives are falling below the standards of the gospel and that they are not a community that is living up to what they preach. He does not want to hear that they are divided in the flesh instead of being united in the Spirit. He does not want to hear that they have given up interest in preserving and propagating the gospel but are only interested in themselves and other things. He does not want to hear that they are afraid of conflict. He does not want to hear that they are puzzled as to why suffering is coming. He wants to hear that, living a life worthy of the gospel, they are standing firm in one Spirit, striving shoulder to shoulder for the faith of the gospel and in nothing afraid – by their courage signing the death sentence of their enemies and rejoicing that they are sharing in the same battle as he has fought. Or we could sum it up by saying Paul is concerned that they should rightly relate to the next world and to this one – to the next world by being a little colony that is already living that way, and to this world by being ready to fight for what they have discovered, to defend this colony of heaven.

There are many churches that are neither of these two things. And they are related, two sides of the same coin. A church that is living to all intents and purposes like any other society on earth, like a club, will not find itself in the battle. Why should it? That church will not find itself under attack. Why should Satan bother with it? There are churches that are neither related to the next world as a colony of it nor to this world in a battle for it. They are simply there – neither one thing nor another. The extraordinary thing is that the more we relate to the next world the more notice this world takes of us, and the more we are in the front line of defending the empire of Jesus Christ. May God relate you rightly to the next world and to this world. May you in your church be living a life as a community which is so different that Satan is attacking you for it, and thus bringing out your courage in defending the gospel of Christ. The Lord sees us as an army standing for the defence of the gospel. Let us respond to the Word of God and ask him to equip us, to put on the whole armour of God that, having done all, we may stand. Then, when the evil day comes, you will be able to resist the enemy's attack, and after fighting to the end you will still hold your ground. So stand ready with truth as a belt right around your waist, with righteousness as your breastplate and as your shoes the readiness to announce the good news of peace. At all times carry faith as a shield, for with it you will be able to put out all the burning arrows shot by the evil one. Accept salvation of the helmet, and the Word of God as the sword which the Spirit gives you. Do this all in prayer asking for God's help.

Please read Philippians 2:1–11

In 1957 I took a decision, which was to change the course of my life. I decided to stop preaching from texts and instead to take passages – sometimes a whole chapter, sometimes a whole book. It is no exaggeration to say that at that point in my ministry the Bible changed and became a completely new book. I did not realise at the time what that very simple step was going to lead to. But within a matter of weeks, out in Arabia with a congregation of young men in the Royal Air Force, I discovered the truth of the old adage that a text out of context becomes a pretext.

If you just take a text out of its setting, you can almost make the Bible say anything you would like. Put it back into its setting like a jewel against a dark, velvet cloth and it sparkles with new life, new light, new meaning. For example, I remember the discovery that 1 Corinthians 13 was not a chapter about love but a chapter about spiritual gifts, and the whole chapter took on a new meaning because I put it back between chapter twelve and chapter fourteen.

Philippians 2 contains one of the most beautiful, sublime little passages in the whole New Testament. I don't think Paul ever wrote any more marvellous words about the Lord Jesus than he wrote in verses 6–11. One commentator said it was like a patch of purple cloth sewn onto the fabric of this letter. That remark betrays that the commentator did not see the patch in its setting. It is not a patch but an integral part of the cloth – part of the beautiful colouring of the whole tartan of this letter. It is when you put a passage back into its context that it becomes altogether different. Taking these few verses out of context, as many have done, leads people into one of two false interpretations.

Firstly, many scholars have taken these verses and made them a subject of theological controversy. They have taken this statement about Christ Jesus in the form of God counting it not robbery to be equal with God but emptying himself, then they have put it in the theological classroom and asked: now what does it mean for our doctrine? They have worked out all kinds of theology, calling it the *kenosis* theory. That is the Greek word for "emptied". A whole controversy has arisen around this one word and they have asked: How much of a God was Jesus when he was on earth? How much of his god-ness did he empty himself of? Did he cut out his divine knowledge of the future? Did he cut out his divine power? How divine was he when he was walking the lanes of Galilee, or was he emptied of his divinity and was there just humanity left? Or was he partly God or partly man? So a lot of ink has been spilled over this passage.

Their mistake was to take this passage out of its context. If you put it back in, you discover that it is not about your belief at all, it is about your behaviour. The question you should ask when you read this is not, "What should I believe about Jesus in his humanity?" but, "How should I behave in the light of Jesus' mind?" That is totally different. Then there are those who have seen in this passage magnificent prose or even poetry about Jesus. They have seen a poem which has been lifted out of an early hymn book. They have said the poetry of it indicates a song. So they have speculated that Paul is actually quoting one of the early Christian hymns. Five verses of three lines, each of them all about Jesus – even in the English you can get the poetry. Christ Jesus being in the form of God thought it not robbery to be equal with God but emptied himself and made himself of no reputation. If you take it as poetry or a hymn, the mistake you will make is to assume that Paul in this passage is trying to lead you to worship, but that is the wrong response to it. Paul is not telling us this so that we might bow down and worship. No, there is something much more practical. This is not therefore a doctrinal passage and it is not a liturgical passage, it is a *practical* passage. What Paul has to say about Jesus here is to lead you to behave rightly towards one another – and that is all. It is to lead you to have the mind of Christ in your dealings with every other member of the fellowship. That is what the context says, as we shall see.

When Paul wrote a letter he didn't stop and say, "Now verse three," and the secretary writes three and writes what he says! He wrote letters as we do, as a continuous whole, and they continue from one chapter to another. You must have noticed that at the beginning of 2:1 it says, "Therefore" or "so". That implies he is following on from chapter 1. We recall that in the previous chapter Paul was replying to those who are concerned that he may be unhappy, those who feel that his imprisonment and his possible early death must be weighing heavily on him, frustrating him, depressing him, and Paul has to write and say that he was joyful already. His imprisonment was spreading the gospel and that made him happy. His impending death could have him in heaven in another five minutes, and he was so happy about that, he could not wait to get there. He was far more concerned about their condition than his own. A slight change in their condition could make him perfectly happy. Here is a man in prison in chains, awaiting the death sentence, yet he can say, "Make my happiness complete." The one thing which would do that was unity in the church of Philippi. Whatever is going to happen to him, the one thing that would fill him to overflowing with joy so that he would be exuberant in that situation and say, "I'm the happiest man on earth", would be to hear that the Philippian church is standing fast in unity together, in the Spirit – that is the one thing that he is longing to hear. So now he begins to spell out the kind of unity he wants to hear about. He is not worried about their Christian beliefs, they are an orthodox fellowship. Nor is he worried that they are getting into all kinds of perverted behaviour – they are not. He does not have to correct the kind of things that were happening in Corinth. There, people were committing incest in the fellowship, getting drunk at the Lord's Supper, but that kind of thing is not happening at Philippi. When a fellowship is orthodox in belief and right in behaviour the big danger is that their unity should be strained. Isn't it strange that the devil can destroy the unity when doctrine and behaviour are right? That is the point at which he can destroy a church's testimony and witness, so Paul is concerned about this.

In chapter two, the key word is "mind." He wants them to have the right mind. Now that does not mean brain, and it does not mean an intellectual or cerebral thing. When Paul uses the word "mind" he is referring to your outlook, your disposition, your attitude, your intention. For example, as you go out of church you might say, "You know, it's such a nice day I have a mind to go down to Bognor Regis this afternoon." That is not a very intellectual decision. It means your *mind* – your bent that way. You see the sunshine, you think of the sea and there is something in your mind making you think that way – this is what Paul means by "mind". What is it that you want to do? What is it that you are feeling after? What is it that you would do if somebody took the brakes off your personality? Where would you gravitate to? That is what you have a *mind* to do, and he is concerned that the Philippians have the right mind – the mind which was in Christ.

In other words, unity is something internal before it is

external. You can impose a unity on people which is no more than uniformity. You can have unanimity in a church meeting: those in favour, those against, none, carried *nem con*. That is not unity, it could be mere acquiescence. Unity is something that comes from inside when there is a certain mind among the people so that the outward expression of it flows from the inside.

One of the problems about ecumenism has been that it has been a search for outward unity without the inward. A better kind of unity comes from the inside as people discover things in common in their hearts – and that unity is going to be the best unity, it is going to survive. It is built on the *motives* of people. So we need a study in *motive*. There are times when you have to allow your heart to be bared before the Lord and let him look at your motives.

Think of a church service. You and others are present together, probably sitting in rows and not fighting. Nobody would get the impression of disunity. But what motive brings people to the service? We would probably find quite a wide variety of answers to that. Some come out of habit. Some because they don't like staying away. Some come out of curiosity. Some come to worship. Some come to hear what the preacher says. If everyone comes with the same mind, then there is unity. But if our motives are varied, then we cannot have unity. We can have uniformity. We can sit in the same rows, but we cannot have the unity that is going to stand when the enemy attacks.

So let us look at our motives, and the first four verses rather take us to pieces and look at our motives fairly carefully. Paul knew human nature inside out and he could look at the human heart and analyse it so perfectly. He starts by making a very powerful appeal to four motives that are present in every Christian's life though they may vary in degree. If there is any of these four things then we have the foundation to build on. If you are not a Christian, none of these things will touch or appeal to you. But if you are a Christian, however young or however experienced, these four things are there, motivating you in your heart, and these are the basic ingredients of unity.

I will group them into two couples because they seem to me to go together. The first motivation of the Christian comes from the second person of the Trinity – Christ. The other comes from the third person – the Holy Spirit. If you are not a Christian, you may nonetheless believe in God. You may even pray to God, but the motivation of Christ and the Spirit are absent from your life. I cannot appeal to them. Paul couldn't either. If you just believe in God you cannot have Christian unity. So Paul is writing about this: If there is any response in your heart to the *challenge of Christ* and *the restraints of his love*. There we have the first couplet, the first two motivations of the Christian. You know when that happened to you. It happened to me when I was seventeen in a sitting room near Tonbridge in Kent. I remember that was the first time that I really felt the challenge of Jesus Christ – not the call of God but the challenge of Christ – and knew that he was speaking to me *personally*, that he was saying, "Follow me and I will make you." Have you felt that? Has there been a moment in your life when you began to respond to the challenge of Christ and realised that he was putting his finger on you, that he wanted you, and that he was going to make something of you? Then I can appeal to you. You have got something that you can build on. You have a motivation that will respond.

One of the effects of that challenge of Christ is to put the restraint of love on your behaviour. There will be things that otherwise you would have done but now you cannot do because there is that restraint of love. There will be situations that you want to run away from, people that you don't want to have anything to do with, and now the restraint of love holds you there. You may not have had much of this, but have you had a little? Have you had this response to the challenge of Christ? Have you had this restraint of his love in situations in your relationships?

If there is anything of that in you, then we have something to build on for Christian unity. If you are not yet responding to Christ, if you are not restrained by his love at all, then frankly we cannot have unity – there is nothing to build on.

The second couplet is the *fellowship of the Spirit*, the shared experience of the Spirit, and the *release of emotions towards others* that brings. Have you had that? Even in a small degree, if there is any of this at all. Paul is saying: if to any degree you have experienced this.... The experience of the third person comes when you are together. Have you noticed that? It is the *fellowship of the Spirit* – when you are with a group of people whom otherwise you would have little in common with and suddenly you know that the Spirit is communicating between you. The effect of that is a release of emotion towards each other of affection, of sympathy – a release of feeling.

I was brought up, and maybe you were, to be so suspicious of feelings that you felt there was no room for them. But I praise God that, time and time again, those who have experienced the fellowship of the Spirit have rediscovered their emotions towards other people, towards other Christians. That is why you may have noticed that, whenever the Holy Spirit is coming down on people, you find there is a greater expression of physical affection and people will touch each other and hug each other because their emotions toward each other are released. Now of course that can be abused and other emotions can creep in. Paul always tells people to give each other a holy kiss. Do you know the difference between a kiss and a holy kiss?

Two minutes! The simple fact is that God made us to have emotions towards each other, to have feelings towards each other, to have feelings of affection and sympathy – to be able to laugh together and to cry together.

If you have had any experience of this, if any fellowship of the Spirit and the release of emotions towards each other, Paul would build on that. Here we have four basic motivations that every Christian has to some degree: the *challenge of Christ* and the *restraint of his love*; the *shared experience of the Spirit*, and the *release of emotions towards one another*. Now we have the basis for unity that can be built upon. We are not there yet but these are the ingredients out of which Christian unity is made. If any of those four are missing then you cannot have unity.

So as we mix with people in other churches, as we talk with other denominations, what are we looking for? Are we looking to see if we can get our ministries together in one ordained ministry? Or to recognise each other's sacraments? Are we looking to see if we can exchange membership roles? No, I will tell you what we're looking for: if there is any challenge of Christ, if any restraint of his love, if any fellowship in the Spirit, and any feelings of affection, then let us build on that. That is unity, and praise God we are discovering that in the most unlikely places.

Now Paul moves from what the basic foundation of unity is to the ultimate ideal of unity: a group of people who are motivated by one heart, one mind, one will, one mutual concern. In other words, the aim of unity is not that a bunch of people should all be motivated in the same way but by one motive. That is what a body is. It is not that at this moment one finger is thinking the same as another finger, and they are both thinking the same as the thumb. That is not unity. What is unity in my body is that one mind is controlling this finger, that finger and that thumb. Motivation of a body is a single thing, not a lot of things running in parallel. The unity to which Paul is calling us is the unity of a shared understanding, a mutual concern, a common purpose. He is describing a motivation that affects everybody together because it is one motivation, not a lot of parallel ones.

When we come together first into the Christian life, we come as individuals but the goal is that ultimately and ideally we should behave as one body motivated by a single throbbing heart, a single mind, a single purpose, a single affection, and that the whole body should be co-ordinated in that way. So Paul defines the ideal of unity as a shared unity.

Let me illustrate that idea by a picture of a crowd becoming a mob. Sometimes in tense situations a mob takes over and there is a mob psychology. A crowd begins to do things that no individual in that mob would do by themselves. Have you ever seen that happen? Something takes over so that the individuals are no longer motivated as individuals. The whole lot often begin to behave in a violent and nasty way. If you could separate them out of the crowd, they would stop behaving that way. So you find that the police go for the ringleaders. What Paul means is rather like this: I want to see the crowd psychology taking over – but not a violent mob, a loving mob. I want to see this motivation affecting all of you together so that you respond to a situation as one person, with one mind, one heart, one will. That is the ideal of Christian motivation: real unity, when every part of the body has the same reaction, the same response to a situation – not because they have got together at a church meeting and discussed it and decided to do the thing together, and voted on it and managed to get a majority on it or even a unanimous vote, but because they are already one in heart and mind and say, "This is what we do." Responding together is the ideal. So Paul has looked at the *future ideal* towards which we are aiming whereby everybody instinctively responds as one to the situation with the same emotions, the same outlook, the same understanding, the same concern.

What is stopping us building on those four things? What hinders us from finding true unity? Here Paul comes down to earth with a bump. There is one hindrance: self-centredness. This is one of the motivations you brought in from your past when you became a Christian. The challenge of Christ, the restraint of his love, the fellowship of the Spirit and the release of his emotion were new motives in our hearts. We are looking forward to the day when our response is the response of one body, with one heart, one mind, one soul. Self-centredness takes some funny forms. There are two which Paul mentions here. I found this a very challenging word to my own heart and I believe it will be to you too. If there is any challenge of Christ in your heart, you are going to feel uncomfortable as you read this, but it will do you good.

Here are the two forms that wreck unity in a church. Number one: *self-importance*. If anyone regards himself or herself as more important than others, unity cannot come about. There will be a kind of schizophrenia in the body of Christ. Somebody is not going to pull with one heart, one mind and one will. Let us spell that out. Self-importance can take two forms. One is more subtle than the other so we don't always recognise it. Behind both forms lies pride – simple, down to earth pride which is "self" written large with a capital "I". The two forms are these: one is to push myself as a person; the other, more subtle form is to push the group to which I belong. Both these forms can be found in a church. I do hope musicians will forgive me if I use music as an illustration. I will then use preaching and other things too. But, by way of example, here are the two forms of self-importance. First there is someone who likes to be chosen to sing the solo because their voice, which is superior to others, may be recognised in the fellowship. That is the personal form of self-importance. "I am a better singer than the others so I should really be chosen more often to sing the solo." But the group form of it is: "Our music group is the best group in the church and is the most important one for the future and nothing is going to touch our group."

It can happen with preaching. A man can preach for the prominence it gives him, for the status and prestige, and often Satan is at the door afterwards. I am not sure about preaching in groups. I am afraid preachers tend to be largely individualist so they don't expose themselves to the temptation of pushing their group always. On the other hand, they can do it by saying, "Ah well, I'm this kind of a preacher – I'm a reformed preacher" or, "I'm a Calvinist preacher" – pushing that party.

You can even do it with praying. A man can pray because he feels that his prayers are the best in the church and his prayers are important and, "If only everybody else could pray as well as I do, this church would really go places." That is the personal form. The group form is, "Our prayer meeting is the best in the church, and if only others would listen to our prayer meeting and pray as we do, then the place would take off." Now behind both these things is self-importance – too high a view of self, either pushing yourself as a person or your particular group.

Paul would say: Let each of you have a lower opinion of yourself and then you will have a higher opinion of everybody else. That is the secret of unity, getting down low so that you are not speaking critically of others as if they are not as good as you are, but so that you are saying "They are better than I am; we need to catch up with them; we need to be following them."

Often, those who are not important in daily life can find themselves a position of importance in church life – they can be big fishes in little pools in their church or chapel. As soon as self-importance creeps in, unity goes out of the door. You will never build up unity as long as this person thinks he is more important than others, and as long as that group thinks they are more important than others. Unity does not come that way. Get a lower opinion of yourself and you will get a higher opinion of others.

A church elder found a real blessing in this – he went out to pick some raspberries from the canes in the garden for Sunday lunch and at first sight saw very little fruit on them, but then he got right down and looked up and then saw lovely clusters of fruit waiting to be picked. As long as you look down on people you don't see the fruit in them. Get down a bit lower and look up and you will see they really have a lot in them that you missed.

Paul was like this. "I'm the least of the apostles", "I am the chief of sinners." Do you know the result of his going down like that? At one time he could not see any good in a young man called John Mark and would not take him on his missionary journeys. But when he is the "chief of sinners" he looks at John Mark and says: Bring John Mark to me quickly ... he's so good for me. Now that is the attitude which is going to produce Christian unity. Any person or group that is climbing up and has vested interest in their own position will wreck unity in a fellowship, but any person or group that is getting down and saying others are better – that is going to produce unity. That is what is going to keep the unity in the fellowship.

The other self-centredness Paul is dealing with is *self-interest*. It may sound strange to you but a church can be riddled with this, and I would dare to say that the larger the church is, the more self-interest creeps in. That is because in the anonymity of a large congregation you can become more self-centred and less concerned about other people. So self-interest says, "How would this change affect me? Is this what I want? Do I like this? Will I benefit from this?" That is self-interest and Paul recognises that you are not going to get people completely cured of that quickly.

So, Paul says, rather than looking after your own interest, consider the needs of others as well. That is very realistic. I would not like to try to build up unity in a church where everybody was saying, "How would this affect me? Do I like it? Do I respond to this? Is this my idea?" There is never going to be unity in such a fellowship. But where the fellowship is saying, "What will be best for others? What will meet the needs of other people even if it's inconvenient to me, even if I don't like it, even if I don't respond, what will help the most people?" – then you will get unity. So Paul is dealing very strongly here with motives.

Now he comes in with the big guns, and if you are beginning to feel uncomfortable so far, what comes next is devastating. *Why don't you behave towards each other as Jesus behaves towards you?* The heart of the appeal in this passage is: have this mind in you, which was also in Christ Jesus. Now that is not a good translation because it tends to create two wrong impressions. One is that he is appealing to the individual – that *each of you* should have this mind. The other is even more misleading – *that Christ is an example that you are to try to copy*. But let me tell you what Paul actually said: "Have this mind among yourselves." Not *in you* but *among yourselves* have this mind. He did not say, "Which you see in Christ Jesus," but "which you have in Christ Jesus." You have already got it. It is part of your experience. It is not that you are having to follow an example of someone outside you – you are in Christ Jesus and you have this already. Let it out towards others. That is the secret of the Christian life, not trying to do what Christ did but letting out what he has put in, working out what God has worked in you for his pleasure. You have already got this mind, then express it among yourselves. For in your relationship with Jesus you have experienced the most astonishing humility and lowly mindedness there has ever been. Let it out towards others.

It is amazing that Christ himself, the eternal Son of God, left his position and put himself beneath you! You have already experienced that. It is a very uncomfortable experience and I hope you have really had it. It is the experience Peter had when Jesus came to wash his feet: he could not cope with it. I look up to you Lord. I want you to be up high, not down there! Peter was very uncomfortable. The Lord of glory – there he is with a sponge and a bar of soap and a basin and a towel, at his feet – Peter's dirty, smelly feet. That is what you have experienced in Jesus. Paul is telling the Philippians to express what they have experienced – let it out to other people. You have been on the receiving end of this kind of humility, then be on the giving end of it too. You are already in this relationship with Jesus, then get into it with your fellow Christians. What an appeal!

So we have at last got to this amazing passage, and the reason why it is so deep, so overwhelming that I almost shrink from dealing with it, is that it is one of the few passages written about Jesus from the inside. Almost everything else said about Christ is written from the outside: that he got in a boat and crossed the sea; and that he healed the sick and that he preached the Sermon on the Mount. But what made him tick? How did he think? What was his mind? What was his motivation? Here is one of the very few passages where you feel you are inside the heart of Christ looking out.

Remember that Jesus was not a man at all before he was born. He was God. He was way up there at the very top. He was God the Son. He had the form of God, the nature of God, the status of God, the dignity of God, the glory of

God. That is where he was because that is who he is. He was at the very top because he was God himself. Then we begin to understand his reaction to that position because we are told here that he did not count it a thing to be clutched. The Greek word means to hold something very tightly with your fingers. It can either mean to grab something that is not yours, to snatch, or to cling to something that is yours that you do not want anybody else to have. It is a very strong word and scholars have debated whether Jesus was not snatching at something that was not his, or not clutching at something that was his. I believe that Paul would be absolutely clear in the answer to that: he did not clutch at something that was his.

Do you remember Adam and Eve in the garden? Satan said, "Eve, you could be like God." Eve snatched the fruit and clutched at it and snatched at death at the same time. I am afraid it is true of the whole human race that we are grabbers, that we want to snatch things, that we want to get hold of things that are not ours. That is the rat race – we are trying to hold things that are not ours, trying to get hold of them and clutch them to ourselves. Here was the Son of God, eternal God with all the majesty and the glory and the power and authority of God, and he did not regard it as something to be clutched to himself, something to be held onto at all costs – he threw it away, stripped himself of all status and made three decisions which are the most marvellous example of humility.

The first decision was to be born as a man and to appear as an ordinary human being. Not a scrap of his divine appearance did he retain. I cannot stand pictures of Jesus in his earthly life that have a big golden halo around his head. Have you seen them? Christmas cards have a little baby with a great golden halo. There was no halo, he stripped himself of all that. There was just an ordinary baby to be seen. There was just a young man in a carpenter's shop. "Isn't this the carpenter's son?" He had no beauty, no form that we should desire him. He was an ordinary human being. He had no advantages whatever over us. He appeared as a mere mortal and by his birth he decided, though he was God himself, to look like any other human being. What humility! Would you choose that? Remember that he chose to be born – we did not, but he did.

The second choice he made was this: now supposing you had chosen to come into this world, what social position would you choose for yourself? Well you can answer that very easily. What kind of schools do you choose for your children? You invariably choose for your children what you would like to have had. The Son of God became a human being with all the appearance of an ordinary human being and then he chose the role of a slave – and that was the bottom of the social ladder. A slave had no rights and no property, and indeed Jesus had none. When he wanted a bed to sleep in, or a boat, or when he wanted a tomb, every time he had to borrow. He was a slave. He chose that level of society. What humility! Still he found a way of going lower. The last right a human being has is the right to live, and when he was told to let that go, he let it go. He became obedient even to death. So his decision to be born as an ordinary human being, his decision to live in the role of a slave, and his decision to let life go – could he get lower than that? Yes he did, even death on a cross.

I do not think you can realise the significance of that phrase because you have never seen anybody crucified. It is not just that it is a painful death. The real horror of the cross was that it was a humiliating death. No Roman citizen would be crucified. It was too undignified, too disgraceful. The Philippians were Roman colonists, they would not be crucified. Crucifixion was reserved for slaves and the most degraded criminals of all. The Son of God died on a cross.

He could not have got lower if he had tried. Here is someone at the very top of existence, God himself with all the glory of God, and he chose step-by-step and climbed down to the very bottom. Doesn't our self-importance and self-interest look terrible? Here is someone who is completely devoid of self-interest and self-importance, stripping off every rank, every right, everything that he could have kept to himself, but he did not snatch at it, he did not clutch it to himself – he let it go. He did it because his prime concern was the good of others – it was to serve. No reputation: Jesus had no vested interest in his own position – none at all, because he was concerned about others.

Now this is really bringing a heavy gun into the Philippian fellowship to say all this. Yet Paul is pleading with them that if there is any challenge of Christ, if any restraint of his love, then make my happiness complete: cut out self-importance, cut out self-interest. Have this mind among yourselves, which you have already experienced in Christ Jesus. Express it now, let it out to each other. Show that you have really experienced Christ putting himself at the very bottom below you. You have not been crucified, not had to go this far down. You have never been a slave. He put himself down there below you.

Within the fellowship of Christ, how are you going to climb up? You can't. You can only climb down in the light of this. This was what Jesus had a mind to do. My glory, let it go. Social status, let it go. Life, let it go. Dignity, let it go if anybody might be saved. From the mind of Christ in the last three verses we turn to the mind of God, and Paul, by the divine inspiration of the Holy Spirit, has not only been able to get inside the mind of Christ but he can now get inside the mind of God and know that God's response to this, God's reaction to this kind of action, is so typical of God who loves to humble those who exalt themselves and exalt those who humble themselves—that is the mind of God now.

God loves to reverse the social order. People who are social climbers – God loves to bring them down. People who take the lowest place – God loves to lift them up. People who strip themselves of their own authority and status are the people to whom God entrusts authority and status. That is why from the very beginning God is the greatest social revolutionary there ever was. He is going to send the rich empty-handed away and he is going to feed the hungry. He is going to take the princes and bring them down to nothing, and he is going to take the nobodies of this world and plant them on the thrones of heaven.

Anybody who is a climber, whether social or spiritual, God will bring down. But anybody who puts themselves down and who realises that the higher life is the lower life and the way up is the way down, these are the people that God can trust, and so with the one who went from the very top to the very bottom, God exalted him from the very bottom to the very top—that's God. That is what he has in mind to do and that is why you can rejoice that there may not be many noble or wise among you. You are nobodies – praise God for that. He is going to lift the nobodies to be somebodies and he is going to bring the somebodies crashing down. That is his way.

So he has lifted him up, highly exalted him and given him a name which is above every name. Now it is not the name of Jesus. He had that name when he came down. That was the name by which he was known in his humility. What is the name? The word "Lord" does not convey to us what it really should. It conveys to us a kind of elevation to the peerage, doesn't it? But it is something more than that. The word "Lord" always has in it the element of authority. It was used of a slave to a master, of a soldier to an emperor, of a worshipper to God. In Isaiah 45, God says, "There is no other God beside me and one day every knee will bow and acknowledge me to be Lord." Paul takes that verse and applies it to Jesus. If any Jehovah's Witness reads this: here in Philippians 2 Paul is saying Jesus is Jehovah (Yahweh). He takes that phrase from Isaiah about Yahweh and he applies it to Jesus. That is as high as God has lifted him. You can now call Jesus "God" again. He is Jehovah and we are his witnesses. It is the one passage that answers the Jehovah's Witnesses more than any other. Jesus is Lord. But I use a little phrase in place of that word because it hasn't got the authority in it: "Commander in chief". That is what it means. The place of supreme authority so that angels, men, devils, all have to bend down. When you recognise and respect the authority of someone above you, then you invariably put yourself below them. Think of royalty. What are you doing when you bow or curtsy? You are putting yourself lower than that person so you look up to them. You are recognising, you are bending the knee, you are saying: "You are above me." When you say, "Jesus the Jewish Messiah is commander in chief," he is above you and you are acknowledging his position.

I finish with one word. Even at the very top, when God has put him right back there, Jesus has no interest whatever in the glory for himself. It is for the glory of God the Father. Isn't that amazing? Still at the very top he wants to hand it all over to the Father. Still he has no mind to grab this status for self to exploit it to his own advantage. This is the point at which you feel like worshipping, don't you? You feel like bowing down and singing "He is Lord, he is Lord." But Paul doesn't let us. Paul says, "Wherefore...." He doesn't say, "Now I want you all to have a good worship and praise session." He doesn't say, "Now I want you to have a doctrinal commission to sort out the theology of this passage." The message is: now work it out; let there be no disputing and murmurings among you.

That is the application of this passage. "Disputing" is open disagreement and "murmurings" means disagreements on the quiet. One is face to face, one is behind the back, but both reveal there is no unity in that place. When there is disputing and murmuring, then what is lacking is the mind of Christ – and I do not mean his ideas on a subject, I mean his *attitude*. So often when Christians disagree they can say, "Well, we obviously haven't the mind of Christ because we have not come to the same conclusion." But you don't need to agree in your conclusions to have the mind of Christ. *It is not his conclusions but his attitudes that are his mind.* It is within those attitudes that you can agree to differ. Have this mind among yourselves, which you have in Christ Jesus: a mind that has no interest in its own position or in the position of its group but seeks to serve and is willing to let anything go in order to serve, and is willing to climb down rather than up – that is the mind of Christ.

So after this magnificent passage, which is a hymn of praise that does lift you into realms of philosophy and theology that are breathtaking, and that makes you want to take your shoes off your feet, Paul nevertheless brings it all down to: *now work it out*. There is to be no disputing, no murmurings, but an attitude that counts others better than self and is willing to let go of any right, any privilege, any status, anything – so that others may be helped.

Please read Philippians 2:12–18

We have seen that Jesus' mind was to climb down and get lower and lower until he hit the bottom – and that is totally opposite to the natural human mind. Now, as we move to vv. 12ff., we could summarise in one statement: *he who was in a position to give the orders chose to take them instead.* That is the mind of Jesus. In vv. 9–11 we saw how he who takes orders is the one who is fit to give them, and God the Father put Jesus back at the top. Jesus took the form of a servant and became obedient even to death. God's way is always to exalt those who humble themselves. The person who takes the orders is fit to give them.

Now here is a principle that runs right through life and is the secret of good relationships. We have an outstanding example of this in the life of Jesus on earth. When a Roman centurion came to him, his servant was sick and the centurion said, "I'm not fit for you to come into my house. But I also am a man under authority and I say to a servant 'do this' and he does it. I recognise in you someone who is under authority. You can give the orders – because you take them you can give them." Every military man will understand that statement: a person who is able to receive orders is a person able to give them, but if you are not able to receive them, you are not fit to give them. That is the principle running right through here. Let us apply it to modern life and consider marriage. One of the problems of many marriages today is precisely that you have two individuals engaged in a power struggle. They have come together as a democracy of two.

The problem is: who casts the deciding vote? The power struggle goes on between two who are trying to establish their will in the marriage.

Now God has the answer to that: it is not a democracy. In the last analysis he has appointed one of those two to take the final decision and to exercise the headship in the relationship. Only if that head is under the authority of Christ will it work. If he is not someone taking orders then the husband becomes a dictator and the marriage is worse than when it started. It is no answer simply to say, "The husband is the head of the marriage." As Paul outlines in 1 Corinthians 11, only if the head of the husband is Christ can he take the headship over his wife and be fit to do so. So if any husband dares to claim scriptural warrant for his headship in the home, then he may only do so if he is under the authority of Christ himself, and any wife would be glad to have the protection and responsibility of a husband who is himself obeying Jesus Christ.

Take parents and children. One of the major problems in family life is controlling children, so eight and nine year-olds are uncontrollable by their own father and mother. Why is it that parents have lost this authority? It is because they are no longer *under* authority. They clearly decide their own moral questions, they decide what they will do themselves, they are not under any moral principles of God and therefore the children recognise they are not under authority so the situation breaks down yet again.

I could apply this also to politicians. The only politicians who will have the right kind of authority are those who acknowledge that they are ministers of God, that they are accountable to God for their political decisions, under the principles of God and not under the mere expediency of keeping in office. But when it is seen that politicians are controlled not by the authority of God, not by an acknowledged standard or principle above them, but by the sheer expediency of getting into office and staying in office, then no wonder they lose the respect of people and lose their authority and lose the control that God means them to have to maintain justice and order.

We can summarise all these things in this word "obedience" – doing what we are told, not thinking of rights but of responsibility; not about status, but service; not seeking to be ministered to, but to minister. That is the thrust of this passage.

Paul says, "Therefore, my dear friends, I am seeking from you one thing – obedience...." His concern for the Philippians was precisely caught up in that word. You see, he had come to them as a minister of God's Word.

Here is an interesting passage from Chapter 33 of *The Mayor of Casterbridge* by Thomas Hardy. Casterbridge is of course Dorchester in Dorset.

At this date there prevailed in Casterbridge a proverbial custom scarcely recognised as such yet nonetheless established. On the afternoon of every Sunday, a large contingent of the Casterbridge journeymen, steady churchgoers, and sedate characters having attended service filed from the church doors across the way to the Three Mariners Inn. The rear was usually brought up by the choir with their bass viols, fiddles, and flutes under their arms. Forty at least might have been seen at these times in the large room forming a ring around the margin around the great sixteen leg oak table like the monolithic circle at Stonehenge in its pristine days. Outside and above the forty cups came a circle of forty smoke jets from forty clay pipes and outside the pipes the countenances of the forty churchgoers supported at the back by a circle of forty chairs. The conversation was not the conversation of weekdays but a thing altogether finer in point and higher in tone. They invariably discussed the sermon, dissecting it, weighing it as above or below the average, the general tendency being to regard it as a scientific feat or performance, which had no relation to their own lives except as between critics and the things criticised.

That is a lovely passage, isn't it? Roast preacher on Sunday afternoon – as if it had no relation to their own lives! Here is what I want to point out: there is only one response which really encourages a preacher of God's word: obedience. Paul is saying to the Philippians that when he was with them he got that response of obedience. To some it may seem incredible that he should write of obedience to him rather than obedience to God. It might be thought that Paul is either speaking as an apostle here, as one of those super Christian workers right at the top among the very few who can command obedience – or it may be felt that he is stepping outside his own limits when he says: "It is even more important that you obey me now while I'm away from you." Let me spell this out. When a preacher preaches, he should not be doing what speakers on television are doing or what public orators are doing or what politicians are doing. The preacher should seek to the best of his ability to pass on *what God is saying*.

Now you may feel it is encouraging to a preacher to be told, "Thank you for the sermon, that was very interesting." A preacher is not interested in whether his sermon is interesting. There are always in every congregation one or two whom a preacher only hears from when they disagree with something that he has said. I am grateful for the letters where they correct me and where they help me to look again to an understanding of God's Word. But where a preacher is passing on God's Word, there is only one response he is looking for and it is neither agreement nor disagreement; neither appreciation nor criticism. You don't know how a preacher's heart leaps when this one thing appears and when somebody says, "You know this morning, God spoke to me and I have done something about it." Oh, the encouragement that is! The Word of God has not returned void. It has *done* something. The Word of God is to be done. Paul was conscious that this was his ministry. So he had poured out words to them. He had given them the message of the gospel but he saw this message not as something to be agreed with or even to be debated, but as something to be obeyed. Notice that Paul frequently says, "You obeyed the gospel. You obeyed the good news."

Now most people don't think of good news as something to be obeyed, but Paul did, because *the good news was God had sent Jesus Christ to save you, therefore repent and believe and you'll be forgiven and you'll receive the gift of the Spirit – that is the good news but it's good news to be obeyed.*

As you listen to a sermon the one question you need to be asking is: "What is the Lord telling me to do?" Some years ago, I was at the door after a service on a Sunday morning and a lady said as she went out, "Thank you for the sermon. It really moved me."

Rather rudely, I replied, "Where to?" She said not another word but walked down the path there with very firm steps and I realised that I had really put my foot in it. I was troubled about that all afternoon, and was at the church door before the evening service, determined to apologise as she came in – and I did.

But she said, "Ah well, I was rather cross with you but I went home and thought 'Well, where *did* it move me to?' and realised the answer was 'nowhere'!"

Paul is saying that when he was with them he got

obedience from them. You don't listen to sermons in order to dissect them as being below or above average. Preaching from the Bible should be God telling you to do something. You obey the gospel, you respond in action, and God's Word demands response and action. It *does* things—God's Word is active, powerful, sharp, and that is what it is all about. Paul is glad that he can look back on his time with them and think of response after response of obedience. Lord, what will you have me to do? Speak, Lord your servant hears. That was the kind of response he got. He is asking them to go on giving that response even in his absence.

The test of a man's ministry is not just how people respond to God's Word while he is there but how they respond after he has gone. It is a well-known test of any man's ministry that the church will show what he has done in the "interregnum". I do not know where that term came from but it is horrible, isn't it? From *regnum* – king, dreadful! But the truth in it is that the Word of God was reigning. The Word of God should have been lording it over people – not the preacher, I hope, but the message. The real question is: do they go on responding to God's Word as much after he has left as they did while the preacher was there?

If they don't, then the power was in the personality of the messenger and not in the message. But if the power is in the message then the Word of God goes on working and the response goes on happening and the obedience goes on taking place. That is why Paul has used that magnificent passage of Jesus who could give the orders putting himself where he could take them and the Father putting him where he could give them.

Insofar as a congregation is obedient and responds to the Word of God, he is able to give power into their hands and to say, "I can trust you with it. You will be under authority so you will have authority over all the forces of evil.

So Paul comes to a statement, which we really must take to pieces very carefully indeed: "Work out your own salvation with fear and trembling for God is at work in you both to will and to work for his good pleasure." What a statement! That is the heart of the appeal of Paul. Some of the phrases in it are very much misunderstood. Phrase number one, "Work out your own salvation." "Hooray," say people, "God has left us to decide our own religion. We can work out our own faith. We can work out our own church life. We can work out our own standard of living. God has left us to work our own salvation out." Never! That is not what Paul means, nor does he mean – and here is the most widespread misinterpretation – work *for* your own salvation. That appeals tremendously to the human heart because it appeals to our pride that we can earn our place in heaven. "Heaven helps those who help themselves" runs the popular proverb, but you will not find it in the Bible.

God does not offer us a "do it yourself" salvation kit! He does not invite you to work for your own salvation. God never said work hard, be kind, try not to do anybody any harm, do a good turn when it's needed and then you'll get to heaven and you can come and live with me – it is the greatest illusion of all. In fact, you can put these two misunderstandings together and you have got the secret behind most world religions. Most of them are people working out their own salvation – both in terms of getting their own religious ideas and in terms of thinking they are getting their own way to heaven. Nobody ever got to heaven by working for their own salvation. Indeed, every man and woman has to come to the point where they realise they will never produce enough to gain admission to heaven. So "work out your own salvation" does not mean that. Nor does it mean – and this is a more subtle misunderstanding – you do it all by yourself *each* of you. That would misleadingly suggest that my job is to work out my own and your job is to work out your own, and religion is a private business and my relationship with the Lord is none of your business. That would be: "I'm working out my own salvation." It doesn't mean that. An English Prime Minister was once heard muttering as he came out of church, "What are things coming to when religion interferes with a man's private affairs?" That is a misunderstanding of our religion.

So when Paul writes, "Work out your own salvation," what does he mean? First of all, "your own" is in contrast to "in my presence". He is saying: I am not with you now – you have got to work it out for yourselves. It is not an individual thing. He means: You at Philippi, I am hoping to come and see you but I may not be able to – even in my absence work it out for yourselves. He is putting the responsibility squarely on them. He knows perfectly well that it is only too easy to become very dependent on a human ministry.

There is a very strong responsibility on every Christian to *work out what God has worked in*. Salvation is not just something that is handed to you nicely wrapped up like a Christmas present with a bow on top that you can unwrap and then put on the shelf, it is something to *work at*.

I remember one of my most lovely presents as a boy. It was from a former prizefighter on Tyneside who had a couple of cauliflower ears and a broken nose, and had spent more time in Durham jail than outside it, and who knew Shakespeare and the Bible backwards because they were the only books he was allowed in prison. I remember how, when I was about eight years of age, he gave me a cheap cardboard box inside which were home-made, handmade tools. The handles were made of branches of twigs and one was a little file, and there was a little hammer and so on. I could have said, "Oh what a lovely present," and then put it on the shelf, thinking, "I've got a lovely present." But he gave me those tools to work at. They were mine. He had given them to me but he gave them to me to work with, and so I began to use them and began to make things, and ever since then I have loved making things with my hands.

Now when God brought you into the way of salvation he did not give you something to tuck away in your heart and say, "I've got salvation." No, he gives you something to work at. Here are the tools to finish the job. God is saying: work it out, apply it.

Now that is one half of this profound exhortation but there is another half, which is very much needed—*trembling*. We are coming across a number of unmentionable words: "obey", "work", "fear", and people say, "That is an extraordinary word to use." But this is the fear that God's purpose and pleasure will not be fulfilled. You see, if God is working in me so that I can work it out, then if I stop working it out, what will happen? Quite simply, God's purpose for me and his good pleasure will be denied to him. That is a fearful and awesome responsibility – that God has left me to work it out. This could be paralysing but there is a healthy fear and trembling that we should have in our hearts that God is working all this in – therefore with fear and trembling work it out. Put it into practice; do something about it.

It would be healthy if you wrote on a piece of paper what God told you to do last time you were in church, and then you did it in fear and trembling lest God in heaven would say, "Oh, there's another wasted Sunday morning. They listened for forty-five minutes or whatever. They heard all those words and what have they done? What have they worked out? What has come out at the other end?" No wonder Paul appeals to them so strongly when you consider that it is to be our prime task to spread obedience – to encourage people to *do* God's Word. "Go into all the world," said Jesus, "make disciples; baptise them..." and then what? Then, "teach them to observe all the things I've commanded you" – that is our task, not just to say it all or to agree with it all or to sing it all, but to *do* it all. I see two trends among Christians today which could be very serious. One is the preoccupation with *experience* rather than *obedience*. To measure a service or a meeting or a conference or any Christian activity by the experience gained rather than the obedience that resulted – "Have you had a good time?"

"Great, wonderful experience!"

You never hear anyone enthusiastically saying: "Great, it led us to obedience!"

For many years there has been that strong search after experience. It is a reflection of a world in which people are chasing one experience after another, wanting some new sensation, some new stimulus, and searching for ever more bizarre experiences. God is not interested in a people seeking experience; he is interested in a people seeking obedience – it is as simple as that. God doesn't mind whether you have an experience in church or not. But he does mind whether it results in obedience or not.

I love hearing a testimony that concentrates not on experience but on obedience, and says: "The Lord told me to do this and I did it, and this was the result." That is a real testimony. "He told me to go and wash this mud off my eyes and now I see." That is obedience.

The other trend is one I hope we can try to reverse: Christians have been preoccupied with the church rather than the world. The result is that instead of working it out we become preoccupied with working it in. We have become almost obsessed with going to more places where more can be pushed in. But what God is looking for in these days is a people who will get together and work it out in terms of the world in which we live – not in terms of what we are working in – until an introverted church becomes an extrovert church.

Why are politics, education, marriage, entertainment, the arts, and one sphere after another of human life in our society, increasingly godless and secularised? Whose fault is it? How did it happen? It was because Christians stopped working it out. Then we have our feeble little protests when we see the results and we want to protest against this and that – and it is because of our having pulled out and become introverted instead of extrovert. We need those who can work out their salvation in terms of politics, the arts and education. Christians need to apply the saving truth and think it through until we can out-think and outlive and out-die again secular society, until we can show we can work it out better than they can.

Let me now summarise vv. 14–16. Spelling out this response of obedience in three dimensions, Paul is teaching, first of all: let there be a ready response to what God is saying. It needs to be a ready response. "Disputings" and "murmurings" are mentioned – grumbling and complaining. Obedience is not much welcomed when it is reluctant, is it?

Do you think God likes it when he says, "Go and do that"; "Go into all the world"; "Go and make disciples", and someone says, "Well, Lord there's so much to do and I'm tired. There are a lot of other things."

"Go and do it."

"Lord, I'm not sure that's the way. I don't see why I should do it all. There are plenty of others in the church and I've done my bit for a few years and I'm going to rest now."

God says, "I don't want that sort of obedience. I want children who are eager, ready, willing"

"Yes, I'll go. I'll do it" – that is what he is looking for, an obedience, a response to working it out that is eager to go without grumbling or complaining. That takes the whole edge off it. There was a time when Jesus said to the Father, "Not my will, but yours be done." And he became obedient to death.

If we obey God willingly, Paul says that we become God's perfect children. In any home, children who are reluctant to obey their parents are not only a reflection but somehow a cause of unhappiness in the home. In any family where the children are not glad to co-operate with parents, there is something that God has not planned. God is looking for a family on earth of children who are glad to obey without disputing, without grumbling, without complaining. "Yes Lord, if that is what you want, we will do it. Yes, Lord, if that is the way you want us to go, we will go."

That is what God is looking for. Why? Because then he can take those children of his to a point where they are blameless and innocent. Such are the kind of children you love to have. God wants us to be innocent children, blameless children, obedient children, co-operative children – that is the kind of family he is looking for on earth. To obey him without grumbling and complaining is providing a family that is ready to go with him. That is a deep concern. As a pastor I look back over so many years and I can see point after point, and I praise the Lord, when he said, "Do this," and the people did it. He led us and we took the step and he honoured that step.

Why does God want us blameless and innocent? So that we may shine like stars in the sky, demonstrating to other people the beauty of going God's way in a world that doesn't like even the word "obedience", a world that is rejecting authority and is rebellious – a world that says, "I go my way," grabbing and trying to climb up the ladder. It is in that world God can say: "There is my family, my obedient children demonstrating in their lives how bright and how sparkling a life is that is obedient and co-operative with Father." That is what he wants.

What a lovely picture of Christians: like stars in the sky.

The sky is so black really that you have to get away from earth to see it properly. When you go out into space the sky goes very black, but what redeems it from being an oppressive, heavy, dreadful thing to look at? Those little twinkling stars. When the stars are out you never look at the darkness. Have you noticed that? They draw your attention. It is almost as if God looking down on so many cities sees crooked and perverse places. He sees people who have distorted life. They have distorted marriage, they have distorted love, they have distorted goodness – they have distorted so much. A perverted and a distorted world – that is the word used here. In that dark and distorted world there are stars – bright lights of obedient children – and people are going to look at them. Those believers are different, they are going to be able to steer a course by them. It is going to relieve all the blackness: you are going to shine as stars.

Then Paul comes to the climax of obedience – if you are not reluctant but eager to obey without disputing and murmuring, and you become God's perfect children, blameless, innocent, shining like stars.... It is old-fashioned to talk like that, but God is old-fashioned. He was always there and he will be there after all the new-fangled ideas have gone. As obedient children shining as stars, the climax to all this is that then you can hold out to them the Word of life. You will never do it without this. If your life is not shining like that, you try and give a gospel tract and you will come very unstuck. The climax to this life of obedience and glad co-operation of working it all out in all areas of life and in our society, is to offer them the Word of life.

You don't get people converted just by shining. You never will by saying to yourself, "Well, I let my life show it." That is essential. But your lips must show it as well. People have to see it first but then they must hear it. "How shall they believe unless they hear...." Faith comes by hearing. It doesn't come by seeing. People say, "Well, I'll believe it if I see it." No, they will believe it if they *hear* it. Real faith comes by hearing, so they have got to hear the Word of life.

Finally, there are two things that Paul, as a person and as a minister of the gospel, questions himself about. Number one: has my life been wasted? Number two, in his case: would my death be a waste?

When you get into your fifties you begin to look back and say, "What have I done with my life? What is there to show for it? What have I done that is of lasting value? How will it stand up to the test of the day of Jesus Christ when he puts all that we have done into the fire?" If it has been good, if it is of gold, it will come out pure and lasting. If it is hay and stubble, it will go. That is the ultimate test of our ministries.

In the day of Jesus Christ, Paul wants to be able to boast and say: "Jesus, here they are. Here are the Philippian Christians. I didn't run in vain – all those sermons, all that preaching, all that exhorting wasn't a waste of time."

But he doesn't leave it there because that might distort the picture a bit. How balanced Paul is! He always says something then balances it up immediately. He might leave the impression that the most important ministry at Philippi was his. This is a very common misconception. I found a brief history of one church where I ministered, commemorating its 125th anniversary. The chapters are named after the Pastors for the periods covered. But that is not the real story of the fellowship. Alas, so many people think of the history of a church that way – as chapters in successive Pastors' ministries. Paul knows better than that. Consider what he now writes. "I look back over my life. Is that a waste? No, but I now consider my impending death. Would that be a waste if my lifeblood was poured out?" Then he sees a lovely picture in his mind. It is a Jewish picture and it is also a picture from pagan worship – when they offered an animal to God in sacrifice, both in the Jewish religion and in other religions, they burnt the meat for God. They gave him a roast joint—forgive the familiarity in the phrase but that is what they were doing. God would smell it and say, "That smells good." Then to give him a little extra treat they would take some wine and pour it on top of the meat to give him a little drink with his roast. It was called a "drink offering" or a libation.

Paul suddenly saw something. It is not just that they were a seal on his ministry, he is the seal on theirs. If his lifeblood were poured out in death it would just be the libation poured on their sacrifice, their ministry, their service. His was the little bit added to theirs. In fact, that is the real situation. The real ministry of a church is the ministry of the members, the ministry of the fellowship. Those who have come and gone, who have ministered to the church, have simply been the little bit of wine that is added as a bonus to the believers' sacrifice, their offering, their service.

So Paul finishes by saying that he and they should take joy in each other. He was the seal on their ministry; they were the seal on his. Isn't that a lovely thought? Because not only in his presence but in his absence they were obedient. They worked it out because God was working in them.

Please read Philippians 2:19–30

The Bible is more of a library than a book, and in it we have all kinds of literature: love songs, proverbs, poems and prose, and we have historical archives. All sorts of media of communication have been used by God to speak to us, but have you ever asked why most of the good news should come to us in the form of letters? Why would God choose that particular means of communication? Not, I think, because we all enjoy reading other people's letters. There is a much deeper reason.

There are two reasons I want to mention, and there may be more that you can think of, but the first is this: a letter is an intensely personal form of writing. It is more personal than any other form. A letter is from one person to others and it is therefore full of revelation of feelings as well as thoughts. If Paul had any idea that he was writing part of the Bible, I daresay that he would have written this letter quite differently. But, as it was, he scribbled off the note to the Philippians and it comes over naturally full of his deepest feelings and concerns and it is an intensely personal document. In other words, it is built on relationships. You cannot have a letter without relationships. It is as if the Lord is saying through Paul to us that the teaching is related to people – it is teaching on relationships.

We should learn within relationships, not as a kind of academic study. I would hate to feel that one day in this electronic age we would have a personal laboratory for each person who worships in a church, so that you sit in your own cubicle with headphones on listening to some impersonal message. We learn the truth of God within relationships. Therefore letters are an ideal form of teaching God's Word.

But a second reason is that a letter usually has a much wider range of content than a paper or an article or any other form of writing. A letter will include vitally important issues but it will also include trivial things. I mean the kind of normal letter people write to one other. Maybe there are some pretty big bits of news at the beginning of the letter, "We're going to move house . . . Aunty May is seriously ill." Then you get towards the end of the letter, "Just bought some new curtains for the downstairs cloakroom and they're a nice flowery pattern," and so on.

You have this remarkable range of interest. You cover most of life in a letter. The little things and the big things get all jumbled up. That is what happens with the letters of the New Testament. In Paul's second letter to Timothy, and remember this is the Word of God, God's revelation to man, there at the end of it we read this sentence: "Please try to remember to bring my overcoat." What astonishing revelation is that? This is the Word of God and God does not waste words. Why should he allow us, two thousand years later, to know that Paul wanted an overcoat? Because God's concern is as wide and wider than the range of our concerns – that is why. God is just as interested in your need of an overcoat as he is in the large issues of your redemption.

So a letter is an ideal form to get the truth of God, which is so intermingled with relationships. A letter, with all its personal relationships, is going to convey that and it also conveys the range of God's interests – that he is concerned with the whole of life, those little things you would put at the end of a letter as well as those big things you would put at the beginning. So Paul writes about Christ Jesus who took upon himself the form of a servant – and that is something pretty big, isn't it? Then, in the very same section of the letter, at the end of the chapter, he says, "Epaphroditis has been ill and he is a bit worried that you are worried about him so I am going to send him to you." There are more verses on that than on Jesus! Extraordinary, isn't it? But I hope that you feel at the end of this study that it is not extraordinary, and that this is God's wonderful way of giving us magnificent heavenly truths and then being very practical.

You find that Paul's letters give you a vision of Christ Jesus who is equal with God and then take you through to the cross, and then take you back up to the glories of heaven and then suddenly right down to earth. He is talking about the most practical outworking and that is why his emphasis in this chapter is on working it out – work out your own salvation. Don't stay up there in the heavens. Work it out down here in very practical terms: in common obedience; in adopting the role that Jesus himself adopted – putting yourself under orders rather than in the position to give them. Put yourself in the role of the servant whose main ambition is to help other people.

I am glad that Paul obviously did not realise he was writing part of the Bible, otherwise it might have been much more spiritual than it is and far less practical. He is dealing with a real situation. He is not thinking, "Now this is going to be part of the Bible some day and they will be studying it in England in the twenty-first century." No, he wasn't concerned about that. He was concerned about writing to the Philippians – that is where his heart was. Remember, the background of the letter is this: the Philippians were terribly concerned about Paul, and the whole tenor of his letter is: You don't need to be, I'm very happy; even if I die I'm going to depart and be with Christ, which is better; If I live then I can help you; everything's fine with me – I'm full of joy but my main concern is you. So he is turning the tables and whereas they have expressed concern for him, he is saying all the time that his concern is for them. He wants to see how he can help them in a very practical way. Nor did Paul realise that what he was saying about Timothy and Epaphroditis would be read for hundreds of years in every country of the world. What would you feel if somebody was writing a letter about you and you knew that letter was going to go around the world and that it would be read by millions of people? It could make you a bit worried.

Well, what kind of a reference does he give to these two trusted lieutenants? It is a remarkable relationship. We often say what a marvellous ministry Paul had, but one of the secrets of his ministry was that he had some tremendous people whom he could send to places, colleagues who worked with him and could carry out what he saw was necessary. So it was a team effort. But when you consider that here is Paul talking of Timothy and Epaphroditis in the warmest, most glowing terms, we have an example of the astonishing change that God can work in the human heart. In the very next chapter Paul says that once upon a time he was a Hebrew of the Hebrews, a Pharisee of the Pharisees. He could not even get on with all the Hebrews. He had to be in an exclusive group within the Hebrews. Here he is saying of Timothy who was a half-caste with one Greek parent and one Jewish parent, normally somebody the old Saul would never have spoken to: he is like a son to me. Here is this Hebrew of the Hebrews, this Pharisee of the Pharisees, saying of Epaphroditis, a Gentile: he is my brother. What is it that takes such an exclusive person and relates him to the most unlikely people as "my brother", "my son" – my family? It is nothing but the grace of God working in the human heart. Nothing else can break down such social distinctions and barriers.

The heart of the message is to cheer up. It is a lovely

thought that God is concerned with people being cheered up. He is concerned with saving us. He is concerned with rescuing us from hell. He is concerned with healing us and with reconciling us, but he is also concerned to cheer us up – it is as simple as that. That is why Jesus was often saying, "Be of good cheer" or, in modern language, "Cheer up." This whole passage is concerned with cheering people up. There are no great problems going to be dealt with. There are no great needs going to be met. There are no big issues to be tackled. Paul is saying: I'm going to send Timothy to you to cheer you up and so when he gets back I will be cheered up. I am going to send Epaphroditis to you because that will cheer you up and that will cheer me up. That is the sole purpose of these two journeys. It is worth sending a Christian hundreds of miles to cheer another Christian up, and that is the message I get from this passage.

That is an amazing sense of values. You might have wondered whether it was worth sending somebody hundreds of miles in those days, long before rapid travel and instant communication, just to go and cheer someone up and enable them to bring cheer back to the sender! Today, in a day of instant communication, that opens the possibility for this ministry to go so much further – the ministry of cheering up. You don't need to go hundreds of miles, you could use the telephone, email, text voice message or Skype. Paul might have had a telephone if only it had been invented in time, but he didn't. So to get that personal contact he had to send someone.

A letter, while it has the advantage of being very personal, has some disadvantages. The biggest is that you cannot see for yourself. How often we have this experience. One of your loved ones is in trouble or ill and you write to them because they are far away and you say, "Tell us how you are." They write back and say, "I'm much better, thank you." You get the letter and wonder whether they really are better. "I bet they're saying this because they think I'm over-worried. We must try to go and see them...." Your desire all the time is to have first hand sight of them – not just to hear something about them but to see them for yourself. Now that is Paul's desire here in this letter: I'm going to send Timothy because though I've heard about you, I want him to come to see you and come back and tell me what he's seen. I want to be cheered up so I want a personal, first hand account.

As we look at these two men whom Paul chose to be his representatives, his ambassadors, I hope we are going to learn one thing about each that will challenge us pretty deeply. I certainly found the study of this passage very challenging.

First of all there is Timothy, a shy, timid, young man by temperament and nature with a delicate digestive system, brought up largely by his mother and grandmother. Do you get the picture? Do you get the feel of this man? Nobody in their right senses would have said, "You'll make an ideal companion for Paul." But God in his mercy put these two men together and they became great friends. Of all Paul's companions, Timothy was the closest. He is associated with Paul in five letters. He travelled with Paul to church after church. They worked together superbly. There is no record of a wrong word between them, different though they were. Now Paul says that he is going to send Timothy to those in Philippi. Paul wants him to come back and cheer him up, to be his eyes and ears. Paul himself could not go, he was under house arrest, in custody awaiting trial, but Timothy could go, then he could return and Paul would be cheered up.

There are two questions about this. First, why is Paul *sending* him and secondly, why is Paul sending *him*? Hope you got the difference between those two questions. I have answered the first. You notice that Paul never makes a decision unless it is the Lord's will – even on a matter like this of sending someone just to cheer another up, so: If it is the Lord's will, I'm going to send him to be my eyes and ears to you and come back and cheer me up. But the more important question is this: why is Paul sending *him* particularly?

There is a large church at Rome with Gentile and Jewish believers. There are many Christians surrounding Paul at this time and Timothy means so much to him personally that it is a considerable sacrifice that he is letting him go. He will miss him terribly during the long journey. Why then is he sending him and none of the other Christians? The answer is both a wonderful and a sad answer. The sad part of it is the challenge to us. The positive side of the answer is this: he is the only one qualified to do it. The negative side is everyone else here is disqualified. He is fit to come, none of the others are.

Let us look at the positive side first, which is the nicer side to look at. Paul is saying: I've no one else like Timothy who has a genuine interest in you. That is a fundamental qualification to find out how someone is. It is no use sending someone who can't feel for people, who is not already involved with them, not already interested in them. Anybody will tell you that. If you want to know how a person is, send someone who is interested in them. If they are not already interested, you are wasting your time because you will only get the outside of it, you won't get the inside. That person will not reveal how they really are except to someone who really cares.

Paul is implying this: of all the people I could have sent to you to find out, there is only one who really feels for you, only one who really cares for you, only one who is already interested, already praying for you, already involved with you, already concerned about you, already able to get right inside you and to know how you are really feeling and what is really happening in your heart. That is the fundamental qualification. You cannot report on anyone unless you feel for them and care about them.

The other positive reason Paul gives is Timothy's *consistency* of concern. It is one thing to have a passing interest in people, quite another to go on being interested. Likewise, it is one thing to have a passing phase of interest in some part of the mission field and it is another thing to go on being interested. Here Paul says a lovely thing about Timothy: You know that he has proved himself to be consistent because as a father with a son or as a son with a father, he has worked with me for the gospel.

We need to think about the relationship of a son and a father to get inside that phrase. For most of us nowadays, father-son relationships are leisure relationships because in most cases today father and son follow different careers, different work, different training. But in the days when the Bible was written, if your father was a cobbler, you were a cobbler; if your father was a carpenter, you were the son of the carpenter. The relationship between a son and a father in those days was not a leisure relationship but a working relationship – in the first instance the relationship between master and apprentice and then, later, a working partnership. It is a working relationship that is described here.

When a Jewish boy became twelve, it was automatic that he moved from being primarily in his mother's company to being primarily in his father's company. It was described in these terms: he is moving into his father's business. Now does that strike a chord with you? The outstanding example of this is, of course, the Lord Jesus himself who at the age of twelve left his mother and went to be with his Father in his business. His foster-father completely missed the point and the message and searched everywhere for him – but in the right place. When they found him, Mary said, "Don't you realise your father and I have been looking everywhere for you?" Jesus was in his Father's business now, in a working relationship – Son and Father. Then, later in his ministry, he kept emphasising this: my Father works until now – now I work.

There are still some examples of this of course in our life today, notably among those who work on the land. Farming and horticulture seem to be the main surviving areas where father and son work together, and father teaches son all that he knows, so that the son starts with the tremendous advantage of all his father's knowledge, experience and skill. I remember at one of the churches where I ministered some rather attractive plastered areas around the auditorium. It was very beautiful, very practical and needed no further decoration. Those plastered areas would stand up to any amount of wear. It was a highly textured finish, very skilled plastering, like the old Roman plastering – in the style of two thousand years ago. It needed to be mixed and then put on, and at the crucial moment it needs to be scraped off just at the right hardness, the right temperature and so on. Those walls were actually plastered by two Italians – father and son who were the last two of five generations of Italian plasterers. It gave me joy to watch those two at work. The skill, the partnership. I have done a bit of plastering myself but it never did that for me – with them it jumped off the trowel and jumped on to the wall and went flat. It was remarkable. I have never seen any other plaster behave like that. But behind it was this father and son team.

Epaphroditus was chosen because he was a man who was not concerned about his own food, his own bed or his own shopping, but concerned about other people, and he was a perfect choice. He is desperately ill and then God has mercy. Do you notice that? Paul says so. It was a mercy that he had on Epaphroditis. It is a mercy that Paul gets him back again. Paul never presumed on any rights in God's service. He never said that because that man came to serve him in God's name therefore he has a right to health and he should give him health. No, when he recovered Paul said that it was a mercy. It was an undeserved bonus. It was something that he did not deserve but God was merciful. That is the proper attitude to health. It is not a right but a mercy. We don't deserve to be healthy. Indeed, the way we treat our bodies and the way we live and the food we push into our mouths and driving around in cars instead of walking, all the things we do, it is a sheer mercy of God if we are fit at all. We don't deserve it. We don't deserve life. We don't deserve help from anybody. If somebody comes and helps you, the response should not be, "Well I did help them last August when they were ill so it's just paying it back." It should be, "What a mercy that somebody came to help." It is undeserved favour. Let us get back to what Paul is going to do about it. He sees Epaphroditis reflecting on the concern he is causing, and Paul knows that no amount of letter writing will remove that concern. He can write and write and say "He's getting better, he's all right, don't worry," but you know what human nature is. They would say, "But are you really telling us the truth? Is he really getting better or are you just trying to keep us from worrying?"

So Paul sent Epaphroditis back. He had not completed his job with Paul, but the apostle felt it necessary in the Lord to relieve their anxiety, to cheer them up, to take away their sorrow. It would relieve Paul if the Philippians were relieved, so Epaphroditis was to go. Again there is a lovely concern for other people shining through in Paul's decision. So he sends Epaphroditis back, but not for Epaphroditis's sake – there is not a word here suggesting it will help him. Some commentators have completely misunderstood this passage. It has been suggested by someone that Epaphroditis was homesick so Paul in his mercy sent him home so he would not be. Rubbish – where is there anything about him feeling homesick here? He was distressed because they were distressed, not because he was. So Paul is using him to relieve their distress.

One final thing about Epaphroditis – his return could be misunderstood. They could have welcomed him with suspicion and questions, "What are you doing back here? Isn't Paul still in custody? We sent you to look after him, what are you doing, coming home before he's set free? You're deserting, you're failing in your job." They could have done that, so Paul indicates that when Epaphroditis arrives home he is to be given a hero's welcome. The Philippians are to welcome him with joy because this man has gambled his life for the sake of the work of the gospel – that is the word literally used. He has staked his most precious possession. He has been willing to throw away his life itself. That is the stuff of which heroes are made. Welcome him home as a hero. Give him a great big welcome. In this way, Paul, in his very tender understanding and sensitive feel for the situation, prepares the homecoming and he will get the homecoming of a hero and not of a deserter.

Let me apply this to you and to me. Timothy and Epaphroditis were very different yet there were five things they had in common, and nothing delights the heart of God more than to find these things in his people. They are very simple. Both Timothy and Epaphroditis were willing to be *sent*. I wonder whether you realise the force of that word. I do not suggest they were willing to go or willing to volunteer, but were willing to be *sent*. What would you feel if your church decided to send you somewhere? Not to ask you to go, not to call for volunteers, but to send you. Timothy and Epaphroditis were sent, and the word is a very important one. It is a word that shares the same root as "apostle" and the word "missionary", which comes from the Latin *mitto*, *mittere* – I send; to send. The church, if it is an army, should surely use this word more frequently. One of the decisions we made when I joined up with the Royal Air Force (my wife joined me six weeks later) was that we knew we could not choose where we were to do our work. We were in the forces, and though it was a little hard at times to accept that, we had to do so. We were sent. I was sent first to Cosford, to two thousand boy entrants. I would never have chosen to start my life in the RAF with two thousand entrants between fifteen and seventeen years of age. Looking back on it, I praise the Lord for what happened but I would not have chosen it. We had married and had got the house as we liked it, and we had just settled in when I got an order: "We are sending you to Aden." If ever you have been to Aden you will know the feelings we had when we got that order, and we were sent. Then we came back two years later to England and my wife went to Lincolnshire and I was sent to Wiltshire. That was how we started our married life by being sent, and not always to the same place. But that is life in the forces.

You get this word all the way through the scriptures. Jesus said, "As the Father sent me" – not gave me a chance to come or asked me to volunteer. Jesus was sent, he took orders and took the form of a servant as a result. "... so I send you." There is an interesting thing here that most Christians are prepared to say and perhaps to do. They are prepared to say, "I am willing to go wherever the Lord sends me." There are not so many who are willing to say, "I will go wherever Christians send me," and that is different. The first leaves me free to say what I think the Lord is saying; the second does not. Notice in this passage that Paul says: "I am sending Timothy to you; I am sending Epaphroditis to you." The word "send" occurs five times in this short passage and it is a key word. Here are men who are able and willing to be sent not just by the Lord, but by the Lord through his servants. In both cases Paul checked up carefully first with the Lord but the orders came through him: "Timothy, I'm sending you to Philippi"; "Epaphroditis, I'm sending you back." The challenge that comes out of that is this: how many are willing to be sent by the Lord first and then by the Lord through his church? How many Christians understood that when they joined a church it put them in the scriptural position of being willing to be sent somewhere by the church?

The vast majority of missionaries in the world today were not sent or told to go by their churches. What happened in most cases was this: the missionary felt a call, the missionary spoke about that call, it was duly discussed – deeply in some fellowships and not so deeply in others – and then a missionary society picked up the call. Then some societies send, and most will say, "I think you're needed here. Will you pray about it and see what the Lord is telling you?" But in New Testament times they were willing to be sent.

The second thing that was true of them both was that they were willing to *serve* – not to be the boss, not to be number one but to be number two, three, four, five, or ten, whatever position they were sent to fulfil. Paul says Timothy had slaved with him for the work of the gospel. Epaphroditis had been sent to serve the apostle, to minister to his needs.

The third thing they had in common is that they were both willing to *sacrifice*. There is not a mention of their own comfort or convenience. Epaphroditis gambled his life; they were willing to lose everything.

The fourth thing they had in common was this, and the secret of it all: both Timothy and Epaphroditis were *selfless* people. I was talking to someone in Kenya some years ago about two missionaries. The person with whom I was talking said of them, "He is unselfish but she is selfless." Very often our main concern in coming to God is our own need, but to be a selfless person is set to be free for others by being set free from self-concern. I sense that both Timothy and Epaphroditis were free from self-concern, that they might be concerned about others and able to help them.

Paul did not divide his letter into chapters but there is a remarkable link between the beginning and the end of chapter two. At the beginning he writes about Jesus as the Christian's model, as the one who took upon him the form of a servant, as the one who was so selfless that he left behind his equality with God and took upon himself the form of servant and even became obedient to the hazarding of his life and throwing that away – that was the Christian's model. I am sure the Holy Spirit put this together and led Paul in this writing of the letter and gave this link: there was the Christian's model; now here, in utterly practical terms, are two model Christians. Here is the mind of Christ and here are two people who had it. Here is an outlook which is to characterise our relationships: putting yourself in the position of receiving orders even though you can give them. Letting go of your rights, rank, prestige and privileges – putting yourself where you are available to help others, even if necessary to throw your life away for them. That is the model in Christ – and here in Timothy and here in Epaphroditis are two men whose mind is the mind of Christ.

Supremely, Christ is our example. It is lovely when you can see good examples in your fellow Christians too. If you think of the patience of Christ, you can look around your congregation and see examples of that patience. If you see the integrity of Christ, you can look around and see examples of that integrity.

Please read Philippians 3:1–9

Preachers are prone to derive great comfort from Philippians 3:1. There are three reasons: the first is that Paul says, "Finally," halfway through the letter and that is a great comfort to those preachers who say, "Finally," and then go on another twenty minutes. A second source of comfort from this first verse is that Paul says that he is not troubled by repeating himself. As a preacher I do get troubled by this, not least when I repeat an illustration. I have preached the same sermon in the same place, and gone through agonies! But it did not trouble Paul to say the same things again because the people needed to hear them again. The third thing is that commentators have been unable to see any connection between v. 1 and v. 2. So, if you have trouble sometimes following me and wondering, "How on earth did that lead to that," I am in very good company – Paul had the same problem.

In fact, there is a real problem. You may wonder what the connection is between the first phrase, "Rejoice in the Lord," and then almost immediately, "... but beware of the dogs." Commentators resort to all kinds of explanations for that apparent gap. Some say that Paul was interrupted at this point by somebody rushing in and saying, "Paul, things are going wrong at Philippi. You'll have to change the letter" – with Paul then saying, "What's going wrong? Write: beware of the dogs" – then forgetting all about rejoicing in the Lord. Others think it has been written by somebody else and added to his letter. All sorts of things are considered to have gone wrong. I don't believe Paul jumped around like that – there must be a connection and we must try to find it if we are going to understand what he means.

We have no problem with the first phrase: "Rejoice in the Lord." Lovely advice, but it is more than advice, it is a command. He is not saying, "Sing a few choruses and lift your spirits." He is *commanding* you to rejoice in the Lord, and since it is in the present tense he means: *keep on* rejoicing in the Lord; go on doing it. Some people say, "But I've got no command of my feelings. How can I turn on feelings of joy like that? I can't." Oh, but you can, provided there is a good reason for doing so. True emotionalism is turning your feelings on when there is no foundation for those feelings, no facts behind it. But if the facts are there on which you can rejoice, then you ought to rejoice. It becomes not good advice but a command.

As a little boy I suffered terribly from nightmares for many years. I often woke up screaming in the middle of the night, imagining all sorts of things were happening in the darkness. One or other of my parents would come to my bedroom, switch the light on, and assure me the facts did not warrant my feelings. Bit by bit they would say, "It's all right. Now cheer up, it's all right. You can see there's nothing here to frighten you." They were constantly trying to lift my feelings by exposing the facts. In the Bible, whenever you are exhorted to have feelings of a particular kind you are given the facts to undergird those feelings.

Jesus was often saying, "Cheer up," but he never said it without adding the reason for cheering up: Cheer up, I have overcome the world. I am on top of everything, why are you under it? I have overcome. It is I, don't be afraid.... It is because of these reasons that we can rejoice. That is much deeper than having an occasional pleasure or a bit of happiness. Rejoicing goes deep. So Paul says, "Rejoice *in the Lord.*" You may not be able to rejoice in yourself; indeed, the more you look inside yourself the less you rejoice. There is not much ground for rejoicing there. Nor can you always rejoice in what is around you. Sometimes on a lovely day, surrounded by the beauty of God's creation, you can rejoice. But the more you read your daily paper, the less you can rejoice in our society. Yet every moment of every day you can rejoice *in the Lord*. You can stop and say: Jesus came out of the grave and is alive now. Has the Lord cancelled the second coming? No, it's still on! Is God still in his heaven? Yes, and I can rejoice in that too. Is his kingdom going to be established on this earth? Yes! Is my future secure? Yes! So you can rejoice in the Lord. It depends on getting the facts right, and when you get the facts right you can get the feelings right, because feelings are best built on facts.

Now that is the opening gambit of this chapter, and it is a phrase that has occurred eight times throughout the letter. In our chapter divisions, it comes in the first half and the second half of each chapter. Four times we have a double exhortation to rejoice – that is the theme of the letter. But that rejoicing must be based on the facts that are coming through again and again.

What are the facts here about these "dogs" and other things? How does that tie up? Very simply in this way: in order to go on rejoicing in the Lord, you need to be warned very seriously about the dangers of those things and those people who would get your attention off the Lord. They put you on to a different set of facts, which are not going to bring rejoicing, they are going to bring misery, heartache, struggle and strain. So, in order to go on rejoicing in the Lord, Paul needs to add immediately a strong warning against people who are teaching something that would take the believers away from that joy by shifting, in a very subtle way, the emphasis of their attention off the Lord and onto something else – in this case onto the law. So he can declare that he does not mind repeating some warnings he had given them in previous letters. He so wants them to be able to keep on rejoicing in the Lord that he is prepared to warn them strongly, in the sternest language, about any danger that would distract them from that joy. So we plunge into this warning repeated from a previous letter which we do not possess. The language comes home very strongly, starting with that phrase, "Beware of the dogs." I once preached on that and said from the pulpit, "Beware of the dogs." Down the aisle walked our Collie dog, Trixie! We then lived next door to the church, and there she was, with people reaching for her and patting her, but a kindly steward removed her from the assembly. We don't have the gut reaction to that phrase "Beware of the dogs" because dogs to us are pets, nice dogs. So for the most part we don't understand this term "dogs". To get the impact you might use the word "rats" instead. How would you feel then? It is a rather different feeling, isn't it? Dogs in the Middle East convey that kind of emotion. You don't keep dogs as pets there – they are scavengers, wild, rabid. I learned this the hard way once when I was driving out in the Arabian Desert and saw the ruins of a town just off the road and thought I would like to explore those ruins and see if I could find anything interesting. I got two-thirds of the way towards them and across the sand when out of the ruins came a pack of savage wild dogs. I am not a good runner at the best of times, but I wish somebody had had a stopwatch on my journey back to the car, which I just reached in time! But I don't mind telling you they put the wind up me. When you see such mangy, scavenging dogs running around eating all sorts of rubbish, attacking people, you give them a wide berth. "Beware of the dogs!"

I have only had one similar experience in this country, and that was at a school open day. The police came along to demonstrate their Alsatians. They needed a "volunteer" to be a runaway burglar. Since I was the only man there that afternoon they said, "You'll do." I faced this Alsatian hound coming straight for me. "Beware of the dogs." It has got something horrible about it – despised, dangerous, diseased. No wonder Jews called Gentiles "dogs" – it was an insult. It was saying "You are out there; you're not going to be in here."

Jesus once said to a Gentile woman, who asked him to heal her daughter, "Should I take the food that is for the children and offer it to the dogs?" A sentence that students of our Lord's teaching have not always done justice to. But the Jews regarded the Gentiles as "dogs" and Jesus called another group of people "dogs". He said, "Don't give what is holy to the dogs". Don't share your most precious and sacred experiences with the dogs. They will turn and rend you. They have no respect for that kind of thing. So Jesus called people "dogs", both Gentiles and those who could not receive holy things. Mind you, going back to that Gentile woman – her faith saw the twinkle in his eye. She said, "But Lord, even the puppies under the table get a few scraps." Jesus said, "For that faith your daughter is well."

Let us go back to these dogs here. Who are they? What are they doing that is causing such damage? Why does Paul speak words which are full of bad feeling towards them? It comes as a shock to realise that he is talking about a group of people who are professing Christians. They are, like himself, of Jewish background. Unlike him, they have not left it behind. They have come over into Christianity with all their Jewish prejudice and they still have it. They still eat like Jews, they still dress like Jews, they still live like Jews. The worst of it is they are following him around. They literally dog his footsteps, and everywhere he preaches they come along afterwards and say, "Paul is giving it to you too easily. He's saying, 'You can belong to God simply by believing in the Messiah.' But there is more to it than that – if you are really going to belong to God you must bear the mark of God's people, and that is circumcision. We must cut your flesh," and they would take out the knives and have a ceremony of "mutilating" their bodies, as Paul says.

Now what was so dangerous about this? It is a little operation, very common for social reasons. What is the reason why Paul is so uptight about these people? After all, when Timothy became a Christian Paul circumcised him so that he would be acceptable in Jewish homes. Well, if he was prepared to do that for Timothy, why is he so upset about them following him around and doing it? For two reasons. One is this: they are doing it not in order to make them acceptable to Jews, but in order to make them acceptable to God. They are saying, "You are not really his children until your bodies bear this mark; you don't really belong." That is a terrible thing to say to anyone. Paul had preached that you believe in Jesus Christ, you are baptised, you are filled with the Spirit – you belong. Here they came along and said, "No you don't. You haven't got the Jewish mark and that is the mark of his people." So that was serious because to tell anybody they don't belong to God's family when they do is serious.

But the other side of it was even more serious: in circumcising their bodies that was the first link in a chain that was going to bind them because it was only the thin end of a wedge. It was only the first law which they were imposing on these Gentile converts, and there were 612 others which would follow it. For they saw circumcision as binding you to the Law of God – therefore, all 613 commandments in the first five books of the Bible were binding on anybody who was circumcised. Paul had been there. He had been under that chain, bound by those commandments, and he knew one thing: that all the time he was bound to them he could never rejoice in the Lord.

Now do you see why he is so upset and why he uses such strong language about these dangerous people? They were professing Christians teaching what they claimed was the Word of God, and they had got it all wrong. They were literally taking people back from the New Testament freedom into the Old Testament bondage. Can you imagine Paul's feelings as he travels around bringing people into the joy, the glory and the freedom of Christ, knowing that he is going to be followed around by people who are going to take them out of that freedom, and bind them up again in all his own past from which Jesus the Messiah had set him free? Can you imagine that? When you have seen hundreds of people set free, to know that somebody is going to follow you and bind them up again? No wonder he says: Beware of those rats – we could call them rats because that gives us the feel.

Then, by contrast, he teaches them: if you really want to bear the marks of belonging to God, just realise that you already do. We already bear the marks. If you want to find someone who belongs to the people of God you don't need to do what Hitler and his henchmen did, going around pulling down people's trousers to see if they were circumcised. If you want to see who belongs to God then look for three marks. They are there in all his people, whether Gentiles or Jews.

The first mark is that they worship God in the Spirit. It is not just that they go through outward worship ceremonies. The world does that. You count up all the world religions and study all the world's worship, and you will see people going through the outward shows. I immediately think of a Tibetan with his prayer wheel. Have you seen a Tibetan prayer wheel with the man swinging it, so that every time it goes around once there is supposedly a prayer offered? If you think that is just Eastern mysticism, let me tell you there is a computer in America capable of offering some two hundred thousand "prayers" a second to God. You can feed your name in and you can go away feeling there is a computer that is doing it for you. That is not worshipping God in Spirit, it is doing it in mechanics, in flesh.

But the mark of the people of God is that something deep inside them wants to worship. They are worshipping in Spirit. It is not put on the outside, it is coming from the inside. The Spirit is releasing them to tell them how much God is worth to them. So they are people who are constantly telling God, "You're great. You're marvellous" – and extolling the mighty works of God. The first thing that happened on the day of Pentecost was not that they began evangelising – it was that they began worshipping. They extolled the mighty acts of God in many languages. That is the first mark of a person who belongs to God and it is a mark in their Spirit, not in their flesh.

The second mark is that they are constantly talking about Jesus, and they are proud to, they exult in Jesus, they glory in him. They say, "Do you know what Jesus can do? He is marvellous! He can do what nobody else in this nation or the world can do. He can do for you more than anybody else." That is the mark of the people who belong to God: that they glory in Christ Jesus. Notice the Trinitarian emphasis there. They worship God in Spirit, and they glory in Christ Jesus.

The third mark is equally clear: they do not have any confidence in the flesh. We need to spell that out a bit. They have tremendous confidence in God and in Jesus, but none in themselves. They will talk about God, they will talk to him and worship him; they will talk about Jesus to others and boast about him – but about themselves? No! They can neither worship themselves nor glory in themselves. I heard of one man described as "a self-made man, who worshipped his maker". What a terrible statement! We are in a society in which the humanist philosophy has got such a grip that we do worship ourselves, and we do glory in our achievements. "We've got to the moon and now we've actually reached Jupiter with our cameras." We glory in ourselves. We worship ourselves. Man is seen as the master of his fate. "Look what we can do now. Anything is within our grasp, and everything comes with microchips." This is the philosophy of our day. Deep down, most people believe in "me" – in ourselves.

People who belong to God know that "confidence in the flesh" has been smashed. They no longer think that they are going to get anywhere under their own steam. They have dropped all "do-it-yourself" religion. They are caught up with God in worship and have Christ to boast about, and confidence in themselves does not have any place.

These, then, are the three marks of those who belong. Now the interesting thing is that wherever those "dogs" went, those marks got changed around and people got confidence in the flesh. They stopped glorying in Jesus and their worship was no longer free in the Spirit. It just turned the whole thing on its head and they lost the main source of their joy.

Paul, to spell this out, becomes very personal. He has got to get this across to them, and it is every Christian teacher's task to communicate it. We have got to get hold of this at the deepest level. We have got to feel the truth of this and not just see it with our minds. That doesn't go deep enough to touch you. But Paul, bearing in mind those he is writing to, approaches this in a way he feels will help them feel what he is saying by giving them his own testimony. He says: "Now listen, I had plenty of reasons for thinking I could make it myself. I had a long list of points in my own favour which could give me confidence in the flesh. If anybody else wants to try this then I could cap his list with mine. Listen to my list. It's a better list than anybody else could write, of things

121

that commend me to God" – and then he plunges into this astonishing statement. "Listen, I can trace my ancestry back through Abraham and his special son Isaac, and his special son Jacob, and his special son Benjamin." You may say to me, "Where is that in the traditional version?" Well, it's there. You have to dig for it. He says, "I was circumcised on the eighth day." That is the first point in his favour, the first thing to go down under the credits, the assets. That means two things. It means, first, that he traced his descent from Abraham, so he was circumcised. But what you may not realise is that all the descendants of Abraham through Ishmael, namely the present-day Arabs, are circumcised in their thirteenth year, not on the eighth day. They wait until they reach puberty. Therefore, immediately among the sons of Abraham, he is special. He comes from Isaac. Then Isaac had two sons: Jacob and Esau. Of those two, it is Jacob because he says, "I am of the people of Israel," and Israel is Jacob's new name when he became the father of the people.

So, Paul is tracing the line down to a third special line. Of all his generation, Abraham was special. Of the next generation, Isaac was special. Of the next, Jacob was special. Of all Jacob's twelve sons was one he had by his favourite wife Rachel – the boy Benjamin. Saul says, "My line goes back to Benjamin," and the little tribe of Benjamin became a very honoured tribe. Do you know one of the sayings in the Old Testament, "After you Benjamin"? Did you know that occurred in scripture? Look up Judges 5:14 – "After you Benjamin." Benjamin was honoured. Why? For many reasons. The first king of Israel came from this little tribe: Saul, after whom this man was named. But more than that, when the whole country was in civil war, and all the tribes were rebelling against Judah because Judah claimed to have the royal line, all the other tribes said, "We don't care if you think you have the royal line, we are going to separate," and ten tribes separated out and had their own king. But there was a little tribe called "Benjamin" who stayed loyal to Judah. In fact, the nearest tribe to Jerusalem was the little tribe of Benjamin. It was always honoured – "After you Benjamin." So, here Paul says, "Look what a start I had in life: Abraham, Isaac, Jacob, Benjamin—that is my family tree." Now, to any Jew that was really one up – four up.

Then he says, "I am a Hebrew of the Hebrews." You see, one of the dangers of being Jewish, one of the temptations of being Jewish, is always to let go of your Jewish culture and assimilate to other cultures. So you become more American than Jewish, or more German than Jewish, or more British than Jewish. That has been a pressure on the people of God all down through the centuries. Paul is saying: "I resisted that pressure. I was brought up in the Hebrew culture. My parents, even though they didn't live in the Promised Land, were Hebrews. They stuck to that lifestyle, and when I grew up I didn't depart from it. I stayed within my culture. I was proud to be Jewish, and I kept it all up." That is one up to him.

We are beginning to move now from those advantages he had which he could not help, which he was born with, to those he could help, which he chose. The last three that he lists are entirely his responsibility. He said, "First, as far as my religion goes, I looked around for the very strictest, strongest sect of my religion and I joined it. I became a Pharisee." I don't think you will have the right response to that word "Pharisee" because of all that we have seen in it, but a Pharisee was a man who meant business with God. A Pharisee was a man who said, "My religion is the most important thing in my life." A Pharisee was a man who said, "What does God want from me? Then I'm determined to give it to him." A Pharisee gave his whole soul, heart, and strength to serving God in the only way he knew how. Jesus said, "Unless your righteousness can do better than the righteousness of the Pharisees, you will never get into the Kingdom." They were well up the ladder.

In fact Paul could say: "My enthusiasm for my religion was so strong that if I saw a possible rival or a threat to our religion I stepped on it. I was ready to leave my own country as a missionary against rivals ... I persecuted those Christians. That showed how much my religion meant to me." In fact, I would say from that little phrase that you can tell how much a man's religion means to him by how much he is prepared to be against the things that deny it. It is not just what someone stands for, it is what he stands against that will show you his zeal, his enthusiasm, his real devotion to what he believes.

Finally, to cap it all, he says, "And as for keeping the commandments...." He doesn't say, "I never broke one," which is what most of us would say. (Well no, I'm afraid we couldn't.) But he says, "I never missed out on one." It wasn't sins of commission that worried him, breaking a law, but sins of omission. Had he missed one out? A Pharisee was meticulous in observing the Law. If he planted a little row of mint in his garden, he measured it carefully. Nine-tenths of the row he planted, and then he had a little gap and he had a tenth bit here and that bit was for God. He observed the Law in every detail.

Now, all that was on the credit side of his life. He said, "That gave me confidence in the flesh." I want you to notice that the word "flesh" covers spiritual things. So often when we hear preachers preach against the flesh we think of sensual desires, but in fact spiritual desires are in mind here. You can be as fleshly in your religion as in any debased depravity that you can think of. You can be as fleshly when you are most spiritual. This is a hard truth for people to bear but it explains most of the religion of the world. It is fleshly religion; it is trying to get to heaven under your own steam;

it is do-it-yourself religion. It is pulling yourself up to God; it is trying to do your best; it is "do your best" religion. That is the major religion in England, often inside church as well as outside, "Do your best religion" – Paul thought he was there.

That list probably doesn't touch your heart. It may be interesting to your mind, but I would be surprised if anyone said, "You know, reading that list really put me on the spot." I can tell you why that is, if you are not a Jew but a Gentile. The culture of our society is not Hebrew but Hellenist, Greek. Our education, our understanding of leisure and of politics, come straight to us through our education from Greece, not from Jerusalem, not from the Jews. Our thinking in Western society is Greek and it is Gentile. Even though we go to church, even though we praise the God of the Jews, we do so with often Hellenist rather than Hebrew concepts. Therefore, a list of Hebrew achievements and advantages does not touch us. In fact, that list puts me off. Does it you? Would you like to live with a man like that? I daresay not. Would you like him to come live in your house and start pulling your mint about, observing all the laws of kosher food and the rest of it? I don't think you would feel relaxed and at home with him. I think you would worry about, "What should we cook for lunch today? What can we give him? Put the pork back in the deep freeze." A man who was like this would not attract you at all.

But I want to take you back for a moment into the situation in which he said this and point out two things. First of all, in Paul's mind this was the highest life that could be lived. It really was. His motives were good. He really wanted to be acceptable to God. His great desire was not to gain anything in this world, but to be accepted by God in the next and to live in the kingdom of heaven. He believed in a future life; he was a Pharisee. The Sadducees didn't, but he did. He was looking for heaven. All the time he was on earth he was living for the eternal. He was living the best way he knew how, the way his mother and father had taught him to live. They said, "If you want to get to heaven, this is the way in," and Paul said, "I'm going that way." So in his eyes it was the highest kind of life. I want to say too that in other people's eyes it was. They might not have liked him or felt drawn towards him, but if you had asked a Jew, "What do you think of Saul of Tarsus?" They would have said, "If anybody's going to heaven, he is. If anybody deserves to get there, he does." That was the opinion.

So we don't have much reaction to Paul's list. When you read it you didn't think, "My, that's the kind of life I wish I could live. That surely must be acceptable to God. That is the life that God requires." You didn't have that reaction because you are Hellenist, not Hebrew. Even the few Jewish messianic believers who may be reading this may have been so imbued with Hellenistic thinking, with our Greek background, with our English education, that they can't see it either.

Confidence in the flesh often comes out at funerals. When I take a funeral of someone who is not a Christian, or with a lot of relatives who aren't, unless we praise the departed, and say everything good we can about him or her, the mourners are somehow offended. If we glory in Jesus or worship God in the Spirit, they think that is not fitting. I have often asked myself why that is. Why do they want so many nice things said about the departed and no hint of what God has done, what Jesus has done? I came to the conclusion it was because they desperately needed confirming in their own confidence in the flesh. They desperately needed some reassurance: "It's all right, you've done your best. You're okay. You're in."

Paul had to learn it the hard way and we are going to have to learn the hard way. You see, the whole picture changes when you put Christ into the mix. When you meet the Messiah and have a personal encounter with him, all your accounts go haywire. The next few verses are all in accounting language. They are all reckoning up, adding up gains, losses, profits, assets, liabilities. Paul is saying: When I settled my accounts with God, when I came to add it all up, in God's presence, and after meeting Jesus Christ, the whole thing went haywire – profits became losses; my assets became liabilities; everything I had put down on the right side became disposable rubbish. It is a remarkable experience. When you really encounter the Jewish Messiah two things happen. First, you want to hide all your bad deeds. You just want to get them under the carpet, out of sight in the deepest sea. But second, you want to get rid of your good deeds too. That is a complete mystery to those who have not met Christ. They think, "But surely, you do your best and get as many good deeds as you can on the books. Then, as to the bad deeds, well, God says, 'I'll wipe out the bad side.'" That is not the gospel at all. The gospel is: put Christ on the right side and everything else goes onto the wrong side and drops out as rubbish. That is the real truth.

Your good deeds can be a greater hindrance to being accepted by God than your bad deeds, and that is a sobering truth. But it happened again and again in Jesus' earthly ministry when prostitutes and crooked tax collectors got into the kingdom, and respectable, righteous people like the Pharisees could not get in. Their goodness was the barrier. Indeed, the worse you are it seems almost the easier it is to accept God's grace, whereas the better you are the more difficult it becomes.

So Paul looked back over all his credits: his birth, his upbringing, his religion, his meticulous obedience to the law, his zeal for God, and he said, "What does it add up to? Profit? No. Loss." Why? Because it did two things to him. It is what all that does to you that matters, the kind of person it makes you. If it makes you a person who is more and more confident in yourself then it is doing you damage because that is doing these two things. First, it is putting self in the middle – self-confidence, self-assurance, self-righteousness, and there is no righteousness so offensive to either God or man as self-righteousness. But if it pushes "self" in, it also pushes Christ out. The more you try to produce your own goodness, the less place he has. The more you are trying to get there yourself, the less he can help you. It is incompatible. If you have got confidence in the flesh you can't glory in Christ Jesus, you can't worship in the Spirit. If you are worshiping God in the Spirit and you are glorying in Christ, you can't boast about yourself, you can't bank on your own deeds.

So Paul changes accounts, and suddenly there was only one thing left on one side, on the credit side – just one word: *Christ*. All the other things he had done went on the other side. He described them using a Greek word meaning human excrement. It was used always in connection with food, and it was either used of the food you didn't eat, the scraps you left on your plate, which were thrown to dogs, or more frequently it was used of the food that went into your mouth and came right out at the other end because it was no use to you. I am sure Paul intends the second meaning because all this goodness had been right through him and had come out no use to him. He had digested it – taken it in and eaten it. He had worked hard at getting it all and it all went out as dung, as the Authorized Version puts it – his own dung.

This is a view of good deeds which only the Christian can have, because only Christ can open your eyes to such a truth. It is the same truth that the prophets saw, as when Isaiah said that our righteousness is to God as a menstrual cloth: disposable. To bring it right home to you, it is as if when we hold up our good deeds to God it is like a little child holding a potty up and saying, "Look what I've done, daddy." You feel ashamed even at the best you have done. It just goes, and what is left is Christ and all his resources, which are now yours.

That is what turned Paul upside down. He says, "In fact, I did lose everything." He did – he lost his Jewish connections; the Jews hated him. He even lost his Jewish name, Saul, and got a Greek name, Paul. He lost his home. But really he lost nothing. Oh yes, it all went, but look what he was left with: Christ, and everything he has. I am rich! Loss? Never, it was disposable rubbish because it was more of a handicap than a help to him. All that background, all those advantages, all those achievements, they were holding him back from the Messiah.

We need to be clear: Paul was not lowering the standards of God at all, nor must we. Because of this passage some have lowered the standards of God. They have said, "You don't need to be righteous now to get to God. You don't need to try any more. There is no need for any more effort now that you are a Christian." That is a libel, a misunderstanding. Let us read the passage just a little more carefully. It says, "My own righteousness I threw away because I had found another righteousness."

Paul still knew that if we are going to stand before God, and be accepted by him, we are going to need righteousness. That is a word you never read in the newspapers. You never hear it on the bus or the tube. Why not? Because we are not interested in righteousness any more, but the word means, "To live right, to do right, to be right, to think right, to feel right, to speak right, to be right." When we stand before God, how are we ever going to say, "Lord, I was right all my life. I was never wrong." If God is going to demand righteousness, how am I ever going to meet that demand?

I think of Martin Luther. So often that theological

professor, a monk at Wittenberg University, becomes such a telling illustration of these things. He went out one day into the country as a Roman Catholic monk trying to work his passage to heaven. He got caught in a most terrible thunderstorm. Lightning was flashing, the thunder was loud and he was terrified. It seemed as if God was shouting at him and saying, "I'm righteous! What are you?" Luther trembled there before God, and he thought, "How can I ever make myself good enough for this God?"

From then on, the phrase "the righteousness of God" was a threat to him. It was constantly banging him down and down, saying, "I'm righteous, you're not. You'll never make it." He plunged into a round of trying to do better. Praying to twenty-one saints every week, three every day, whipping himself in a cell until he fell unconscious to the floor – trying to beat righteousness into himself and beat out evil by punishing himself, and striving harder and harder; going on pilgrimages to Rome, going to visit relics. He tried the lot. It is sad that still there are many trying that same kind of road.

Then one day, in his Bible studies in Paul's letter to the Romans, he came across that phrase again – "the righteousness of God" and he saw it completely differently. He saw it not as a threat but an offer. He saw it as God saying, "Here is my righteousness for you, stop trying to get your own. I have enough for both of us. Here is my righteousness, you don't need your own, here's mine." The righteousness of God became, for Martin Luther, that with which God would make him righteous so he did not need to make himself righteous. Isn't that a thrilling discovery? It is the heart of being converted. It is the heart of coming to Christ. It is the heart of believing that all the good things you have ever done have got you not an inch nearer to heaven. They may have made it harder for you to get there because you are going to need the righteousness of God himself to get there. He is willing to give it, and he wants to share it. Isn't that an amazing truth?

We have come full circle. Paul began by saying, "Rejoice in the Lord." Now you can rejoice because by faith you have the righteousness in the Lord that you need. Circumcision leads you back to struggling and striving in this meritocracy in which we live. We are so flooded with the idea: "Do your best and leave the rest." But that is going to get you nowhere towards God. It may get you the approval of men, but not of God. God needs a righteousness that is far exceeding that of the Pharisees, way above those who do their best. God wants a righteousness the same as his, and he is prepared to give it to those who believe in his Messiah, his Jesus.

What is your biggest need now? Do you need peace? Don't try and get peace yourself, I beg you. There is enough peace in Jesus for you. Do you need wisdom? Don't try and be clever, there is enough wisdom in Jesus for you. Do you need strength to resist? There is enough strength in Jesus for you. What do you need? Don't try and do it yourself; don't try and work it up. Appropriate it in Christ. He is our wisdom, he is our righteousness, he is our all in all – you have everything when you have him. You have all the resources you need. It is liberation. It took a miserable Pharisee called "Saul of Tarsus", struggling to get to heaven, and it set him free from that struggle and said, "Here is my righteousness", and Paul could rejoice in the Lord. It is a revolution.

There are those who would say: If you teach this, you will undermine all moral motives. You will get people saying, "Oh well, I needn't try to be good. I needn't bother at all." You will get them sitting back in their pews, complacent, content. Well, if we stopped at 3:9 that could happen. But Paul never lets that kind of wrong conclusion be drawn. In the next passage he says: I don't count myself yet to have arrived. I have not yet appropriated all that God has for me when he laid hold of me. I forget everything that is past, my failures and my successes and I strain every nerve and I press on toward the goal.

Paul did not cease to be an ambitious believer but he pressed toward the goal and now he was going such a different route. Somebody said that he was teaching that instead of climbing the stairs to heaven you go up in the lift. I do not think that is a good analogy. He had once been climbing a set of stairs which never reached the top floor, and therefore was a waste of time. But now he was going to climb another staircase. He was going to reach up for every bit of Christ's righteousness that he could have. He wanted everything that Christ had for him. That is a different kind of striving, a different kind of reaching – a different kind of struggle altogether. It is one that is rewarding and it is one that at every stage leads to further rejoicing and not the misery of saying, "Will I ever make it?"

Please read Philippians 3:10–21

When you spell out the gospel in its true meaning you are bound to get a double reaction. It depends very much on whether you feel you need help or not. If you are self sufficient, if you are an independent person, if you feel, "I can make it on my own, thank you; no, don't help me, I'll manage" then the gospel is offensive because it says that all your self-effort is wasted when it comes to God. All your good deeds are not going to help you one little bit towards heaven. That really crushes us, and pride is the problem. We like to be independent, we like to manage on our own; we don't like to be helped along. This applies not only to horizontal relationships to other people, but to our vertical relationship with God.

I think the biggest concession natural man makes to God is this: "I'll make it as far as I can on my own Lord, and you can just take me the last little bit." Then I keep my self-respect – I got most of the way myself. God will have none of that. He helps us all the way or not at all. If we choose to go to heaven in a "do-it-yourself" way then we will not get there because the very best of which I am capable is not good enough for God. It is not good enough for heaven and it is not good enough for you either. Would you like to live with me forever in heaven until I am perfect? Even the slightest sin in me could be a profound eternal irritation to you in heaven. No, I am not even good enough for myself, however hard I try.

Now we need to look at the two major misunderstandings

which come from this teaching. People are very quick to point them out. The first conclusion is the highest wrong reaction, and the second is the lowest. They only differ in degree. At its best, the wrong reaction to this teaching is: "Well, it doesn't matter. I don't need to try any more to be good." In other words, it is the danger of moral and spiritual lethargy, of settling down, saying "Fine, all I need to do is step onto the lift marked 'salvation', press the top button marked 'heaven' and wait, and some day in the future I will suddenly arrive at the penthouse and there we are. The angels will welcome me as I step off the lift." It means that people make little progress in the Christian faith – they get stuck. If they give their testimony they have to go back to their conversion because very little has happened since then.

That is comparatively a milder form of another error, which is more severe, but both are wrong deductions. The second is the danger of *licence*. On the one hand there is indolence, on the other hand indulgence. On the one hand settling down and saying, "I don't need to make the effort," on the other hand: slipping back and saying, "It doesn't matter how I live at all."

The latter is the more dangerous, and yet both are wrong. Both share the same idea that my own state no longer matters. That is the root error in both these deductions. They are both assuming that, because God is not asking me for my righteousness but giving me his, my state is a matter of indifference to him – that it does not matter how good I am or how bad I am.

So in the second, more severe form, people say, "Forgiveness is a blank cheque to do anything I want." There were even those who listened to Paul preaching and said, "You know the logical deduction of that – it is, 'Let's sin some more because it gives God a chance to give us more grace.'" Let's sin that grace may abound. What an incredibly devilish argument, which turns morality upside down, and wrong way around and inside out. But it is saying, "Let's sin that grace may abound." Are you really teaching this, Paul?

In the rest of chapter 3, he corrects any wrong impressions that may be left by the first half. In fact, the Bible always does this. If it makes a point strongly, it usually balances up straightaway to correct any false impressions that may be left. The balance in the Bible is beautiful. Every truth has its counterbalance. As I have already pointed out, there is a problem when you take a bit out, taking a text out of context and you make it a pretext. Take any part of the Bible, rip it out of its context, and you can prove anything you like. But put it back in and look around it and you will see the balance. Paul was conscious that what he was affirming could be misunderstood.

How do people get these wrong ideas when they hear the gospel preached? How do they jump to wrong conclusions? The answer is very simple: they do so by logic rather than life. Very often our logic will tell us one thing, but in fact life works out quite differently. You may have heard of the aerodynamics expert who spent some months proving that aerodynamically a bumblebee cannot fly. Logically he had all the formulae worked out, he had every bit of proof that he needed – but then in life the bumblebee just got on flying. In the same way, people take doctrines of the Bible, and their logic draws deductions. The classic case is predestination. Oh, what logic doesn't do with that! It is true that God predestined us before the foundation of the world, our names were written in that book of life. But then people say, "Well, if God predestines, then this and this..." and their deductions are all logical but they are not life. When you live in God's predestination it is quite different from the logic. In this case there are false deductions that if you teach that our righteousness gets us nowhere, you introduce lethargy and licence. You will have people settling down, or even worse, slipping back into their old life. That may be thoroughly logical but it is not life. Those who welcome the good news of the gospel that they can have a righteousness that is not their own – a righteousness given through Christ by faith – you will find that the effect on them is the opposite of logic. Life does not work out that way.

Therefore Paul is going to answer these two dangers by talking about life. He is not going to have some intellectual debate with those who draw the wrong conclusion. What he does is first to refer to his life. Is that how it worked out when I threw away all my good deeds? Then he looks at other people's lives – those who had heard him and had put into practice what he preached, and those who had really lived it out. You see what happened in their lives. There is a pattern there for you to follow and it is not the pattern of lethargy, and not the pattern of licence. Life does not operate according to logic and I am rather glad about that because those of us whose intellects are not very bright can still grasp life when the logicians argue about it.

How do people get it wrong by logic rather than life? That is why Paul has to say: If you are thinking differently from me then God will have to make it clear to you. God himself will have to reveal some new truth that will put you right. There is a profound truth in this: that when logically someone is wrong it is very rarely that you can argue them out of that position. It really requires God to come into their mind with a new revelation. Then they will think: "How did I miss it before?" Have you noticed that again and again? When I have argued with students, for example, about the Christian faith, I have found that as soon as I answered one argument, they switched to another. As soon as I answered that they were onto another and it just went on and on.

I was in a school one day and it went on for about forty

minutes, one question after another. They weren't really wanting their questions answered, they were trying to find a question I couldn't answer and I could see this. Having spoken to the sixth form pupils and the staff for an hour, I said, "Any questions?" There was silence and then a boy came up with an old chestnut and after he had asked it, he signalled to his pals. I realised there was a battle so I said, "What's your name?" He said, "Derek." "Right," I said, "Derek," and I began to talk to him as if there was nobody else in the room, which rather helped. But you see he was not really interested in getting an answer. Logic will switch from one argument to another. You realise with that lad and with others, God will have to put them right. God will have to step in and show them that their logic looks so silly to him. What must God think when somebody comes up with the question, "Who made God?" It sounds such an illogical question, and such an unanswerable argument. It is such a silly question to God. It is like asking, "How do you have a square circle?" It is nonsense because God is eternal and therefore he cannot be made.

You must live according to the light you have already received and then you will understand the next bit. That is a profound truth. You don't understand more of Christianity by logic. You understand more when you live it. So Paul doesn't argue in the rest of this chapter, he says in effect: Look at life. Let's see how life works out.

How then does Paul put right these two wrong assumptions? The answer is by placing them in the context of two historical events, which forever prevent you from reaching those two conclusions: namely, the cross and the resurrection of Jesus, which come all the way through the rest of the chapter. All those logical deductions which seemed so clear, so reasonable, when you put them beneath an occupied cross and outside an unoccupied tomb, lose the power of argument.

They are shown up for what they really are in the light of these two fundamental facts at the heart of the gospel of Jesus: that he died for our sins and that he rose again on the third day. These two facts keep us on course.

Paul now plunges into autobiography. What effect did it have on him to know that all his good deeds were wasted, rubbish, muck, to be disposed of, to be thrown away? He lost the lot – his Jewish background, his law keeping. He lost everything when he got Christ. Paul found the pearl of great price, and so got rid of everything else. But what happened when he found the pearl? Did he settle back? Did Paul sit down? Did he look for a nice, little place to retire on the coast of Asia Minor where he could sit and watch the sea and praise the Lord that one day he would get to heaven? No – Paul had not changed his ambition, nor had he slackened his effort one little bit.

We have really got to be careful to see what did change in Paul and what did not alter. Here are two things that did not change when he met Christ. First, his ambition to be righteous in God's sight had not changed. He knew still that anybody who is going to be approved by God and is going to live with God *must* be righteous. That is what he had been trying to get to in his Jewish observance of the law. In all his efforts as a Pharisee and a Hebrew that is what he had been after, and he had not got it that way. Now he can get it but he is still as determined to have it as ever he was. So his goal had not changed. He still wanted to be righteous and he was still going after that with every part of his being.

The second thing that had not slackened was his *effort* to get there. He is still this ambitious man who is going to go after this one thing. He is going to go after it with all his might and main. Talk about settling down? Talk about lethargy? The next few verses knock that right on the head.

You see, I want to draw some rather careful distinctions –

they are not logical, they are life and you must take them as experiences of life. Here is the first: a*ll God's righteousness may be credited to you without your appropriating any of it*. That is a very important distinction to get hold of. I must use a very simple, perhaps silly, little illustration to get it across. Supposing you saw me walking down the High Street in rags, and supposing you could see I had not had a square meal in months, and supposing you knew that I was in debt to a whole lot of people around town and could not pay the debts because I was bankrupt, and you said to me, "Brother, I'm so sorry for you. I want to help you." You went to my bank – a bank that I would no longer dare to go to, and you went in my name and you put a large sum of money into my account, saying to the bank manager, "Credit that to him so that he can live differently." Suppose then that you met me a month later still in rags, and I was marching down the High Street saying, "Hallelujah, my bank balance is right!"

You say, "Just a moment. What are you wearing rags for?"

"Oh."

"Have you paid any of your debts off?"

"No."

"So why are you living like this?"

Are you beginning to get the message? God could say: Your righteousness is no good, but mine is enough for both of us. In your heavenly account, everything of mine is down on your credit side. All that there is in Christ is down as credit – all his righteousness, all his wisdom, it is yours. But I don't see you using any of it on earth. How strange. You are singing about it, you are talking about, but you are not using it.

Paul realised that the moment he believed in the Messiah Jesus, everything in Jesus was credited to him. All the other things dropped off on the debit side. He did not mind them going because by then he counted them as rubbish. But what was left was Christ with all the fullness of the godhead in him bodily, and there was everything he needed. But Paul wanted it on earth as well – now. That is the first paradox we need to grasp: though all the righteousness of Christ has been given to me, I may not be taking it. Though from God's point of view it is down on my bank balance in heaven, nevertheless, from my point of view in daily life I am not touching it. Paul had switched his ambition to grasping all the righteousness that was in Christ—that was what he wanted now. He had been trying to grasp his own, but he did not want any of that any more. Now he wanted to be a maximum believer and not a minimum believer. A minimum believer says, "What's the minimum I need to be a Christian? How little can I get by with? How infrequently can I go to church and still be kept on the roll?" A maximum Christian says, "How much can I have? How often can I go? I want the lot."

The second paradox I want to try to explain is that although the righteousness is all ours in Christ, and we need to appropriate it, it will never be *ours*. It cannot be transferred from him. Righteousness is not a kind of thing you can parcel up and pass from one person to another. It is always *his* righteousness, it will never be mine in another sense. It can only be mine in experience. Not as I get it out of him and into me, but as I get into him – that is the difference. Or to put it in a much simpler way, you cannot have anything of Christ's apart from a more intimate relationship with him because it stays in him. You cannot live a long way away from Christ and have anything of his. The nearer you get to him, the more you can have of his, because it is his and it stays in him. So Paul's ambition is to know him and be found in him, to be right there where those resources are his, not because they are in Paul, but because Paul is in Christ. Do you see the difference? It may not sound sensible or reasonable, but it is life. You know that this is true even at the human level. Therefore Paul wants to get close enough to this person of Jesus Christ to experience the power of his resurrection, to feel what he felt after he had burst the bands of death, to have that sense of vitality, victory, calm and poise that meant he knew that no enemies could touch him. Paul wanted it *now*. He knew that the only way to it is a relationship. Whereas once Paul's ambition was to keep the laws in order to be righteous, now his ambition is to know Jesus in order to be righteous, and to know him so well that he feels the power of Christ's resurrection quickening his daily life.

Paul felt that he was living already the right side of the grave – living in the kind of victory that he enjoyed after he died to sin and was alive to God. He wanted to appropriate that. Very honestly, he recognises that in a really deep relationship, if you are going to have an intimate knowledge of someone, you have to share their pain as well as their joy. So he says, "I want to share his sufferings and become like him in his death so that he can lift me out of the dead. I can be resurrected out from the dead, and be living as a resurrected life now." He realised that there is no shortcut to resurrection. You cannot rise from the dead until you die. If you are going to know Jesus and know him inwardly, it is not by being crucified on a cross. Paul could not be crucified, he was a Roman citizen. But it is by going through what Jesus went through in his death that you know what Jesus knew in his resurrection.

What did he know in his death? Well, he knew all the pain of struggling with sin. He knew all the loneliness and hurt of being rejected by men. He knew the anguish of carrying in his own spirit the weight of the guilt of others. He knew all that, and Paul says, "I want to know that too. I want to experience that." What was Jesus doing on the cross? Ultimately, you can say he was letting go any rights to his life that he had. We die hard, we struggle to keep a bit of our own life, we have a vested interest in our own existence, so being crucified comes hard. But Paul knew that unless he went through the pain of giving up every right to every part of himself, including his life, he could not know the power of the resurrection. So he wants to get closer to Jesus, and closer to him in his death and resurrection – that is his new ambition. He knows that he can therefore live a resurrected life here and now.

Resurrection is not just something that is going to happen to him in the future, it is for now – that is the secret of the Christian life. We are not to try to emulate Jesus during the days of his flesh before he died; we are to be living in his resurrection after he died. That is why the sign of beginning the Christian life is baptism, which goes through a death and a burial – and then being raised to walk in newness of life. It is saying right from the beginning: We are going to live the right side of the death and resurrection of Jesus: enter into this, and it is the way.

You see, most people who do not understand the gospel assume from what they learned in Sunday school, or picked up in church, that all we are saying is: "Jesus lived a good life – try to imitate him; do your best in the light of what he did." But no, it is much more than that. The focus is not on his life, but on his death and resurrection, "That I may know him". This was Paul's ambition: no lethargy, no settling down.

Paul is a go-getter of the first order. Here he is saying an amazing thing: even though all the righteousness of God is now attributed to him, he does not count himself as having arrived. He is on the right road but has not got there yet. That is quite a statement because as a Jew he would have said: As touching the Law, faultless – I've arrived; I'm there. But as a Christian he knew he was not there, he was still running.

He then puts it in a delightful way in v.12 – when Jesus chased after me, captured me, and [literally] laid his hands on me to arrest me, he must have done it for a purpose. Why get hold of me? He must have done it for something. My ambition is to chase after, and capture, and lay my hands on that for which he laid his hands on me.

Do you see his response to Jesus? Just ask yourself why Jesus got hold of you? Why did he stop you in your tracks as he did? Why did he steal into your life as he did? Why did he confront you with himself until finally you surrendered? What purpose had he in mind? Just to get you to heaven? No, he did it because he had something for you on earth. It is not just that he gave you a ticket and said, "Some day, when you die, use that and you will land up in a room that I have got ready for you." That is only part of the gospel, but the gospel begins immediately. He put his hands on us so that we could start living now and have eternal life now. It does not come automatically because you have been converted. It is something for you to take hold of now as he took hold of you.

There is a fascinating little word in the Greek here. Paul, describing earlier his Jewish life, said, "As touching zeal, persecuting the Christians." The Greek word for "persecuting" there is "to chase after and capture". Now he talks in exactly the same language, uses the same word, about Christ. He is declaring: Whereas once I was running after Christians to grab them, now I am running after Christ to grab him. That is the only difference – not lethargy, but running after a different target. The goal is now not grabbing the Christians and putting them in prison, it is grabbing Christ and putting Christ in himself. That is what he is after, so his ambition comes through very strongly.

You can tell a man of ambition. He has two marks: concentration and determination. *Concentration* – he cuts out those things that are irrelevant to his goal. He strips off, he limits; he narrows his life. A man with ambition lives a narrow life. Paul did. "One thing I do" – just one thing, not a whole lot of things. All of his life gears to this one ambition. Everything somehow contributes to it – Paul is a single-minded person now. To do that, do you know what you have got to do? You have to exercise your "forgettery". One of the reasons why we are not concentrated in our living is that we remember the past too much. You can remember your past failures on one hand, or your past successes on the other, and both of them will confuse this concentration. Anybody looking back loses concentration. You try ploughing with a couple of horses and a single furrow plough. You lose your concentration and your eye gets off that tree at the far end of the field, you look back to see how you are doing – then see what happens very quickly without you realising it!

Concentration demands that you forget the things that are behind. Oh, you may have had some terrible failures in your Christian race. You may have had some terrible mistakes. Forget them! God has. As soon as you mentioned them to him he forgave and forgot them. Forget them and forget those successes – those things you did well – please forget them too. Or else you will live in them, you will rest on them. Forget your past achievements. Can you imagine an athlete running around a race track who keeps looking back and saying, "Ah, there's the fifty-yard mark, I got past that well," running a bit then saying, "There's the hundred yard point, I got past that, didn't I? I was going like a bomb." You don't win the race like that. You win the race by keeping your eye on the finishing tape. So Paul has concentration, forgetting all that lay behind and going for the goal.

Secondly, Paul is so *determined* that he stretches every muscle and nerve to get ahead and grab that goal. It is a picture taken from the foot races of Greece and Macedonia, which were very common. Sport was popular. You get the picture of the man whose sinews are sticking out through his skin and whose muscles are tense, who is sweating and is straining every nerve, until you feel that he will collapse if he does get there. It is a picture of an athlete. You see, Paul knew that when God called him he was calling him to a life that was so much higher than the life he was living. He knew that he had to run for it, that he had to grasp it, and that he would not have it in this world unless he went all out for it. So Paul is saying that he is flat out for the finish.

Then he shows his readers it is a mark of Christian growth that you are increasingly dissatisfied. This is true of other parts of life. It is true of athletics and it is also true of art; it is true of science and it is true of so many other spheres, that the nearer you get to perfection, the harder you try. The nearer you are to your goal the more you are aware that you are not there. It is those who are at the beginning of it who are not aware of the gulf. With every human effort, the nearer you get to your goal the more you say, "Oh no, that's not good enough – I am going to try harder." An artist who was asked which was his best picture said, "My next." That meant he was a pretty good artist. He had got a long way and so he was pressing on. How true it is of Christians: the more you have progressed, the more mature you are, the more you will say (and not just say but believe): "I've got a way to go yet; I have not arrived; I am not living the fully resurrected life yet, but I am pressing on." It is the mark of maturity.

The second danger is licence – slipping back; indulgence. Some have said, "Well, if all the righteousness is God's, I can be unrighteous; if he forgives, I can sin. If his grace covers evil, I can be evil." It is a wicked argument and Paul is going to deal with it. He still talks about his own life, but he now brings in others' lives and uses them as an argument. His readers are invited to look at what happens to those who draw the wrong deduction and then live by it. I can imagine at this point Paul dictating the letter, his voice choked, his eyes filled, and tears beginning to roll. I can imagine his secretary or amanuensis looking up and saying, "What's got into him?" All his letter has been full of joy and rejoicing – 'I'm so happy and you should be happy too' – and suddenly he's crying. Why?" Because Paul had many failures in his evangelism. I do not know whether we should find that a comfort or not, but Jesus knew rejection of his message too. Jesus said when he preached that so much falls on hard ground, stony ground, among the weeds, and nothing comes of it. Paul had the experience – as every preacher and every evangelist has – in his case of many who welcomed the gospel apparently, who thought it was good news that God could give them righteousness and enough. They professed faith, and they would have been ready to call themselves Christians, but the sad truth was that their logic got hold of them and they did not live it. Their logic said, "Now that we're on our way to heaven we can live how we like. We can do what we want to, we're safe." When you say you are saved you have to ask two questions: "What am I saved *from*?" and "What am I saved *for*?"

So we have this situation that they did not live it out. Their logic ran away with them. Their logic said, "Fine, we can do what we like now." Paul, weeping over these many failures, is saddened that people could come so near to the truth yet twist it with the most awful effects in themselves. Can anything be more painful than having got somebody interested in the gospel and to a point of commitment to it, then to see that they had missed the heart of it, and that their life did not follow through and their logic took over? The point he wants to make is that these people's lives are now such an utter contradiction to the gospel that you cannot possibly say, "This is a deduction from the gospel." They are so inconsistent that they are illogical and anybody can see it.

He says five things about them. Firstly, they have become enemies of the cross. Why enemies? Because they are denying the very reason for which Christ died, and they are undoing all that he died to do. Christ did not die to give people liberty to sin; he died to give them liberty not to sin. Christ did not die that people might go on living the lives they were living, but he died that they might live a higher life because in their deepest heart they surely wanted to. Christ did not waste his sacrifice, but these people, in drawing this wrong deduction and living like that, are in fact throwing all of Christ's sacrifice away.

Secondly, he says about them that their end is destruction. In other words, their way of life has become a way of death. They are doing all those things that are ultimately self-destructive. They will finish up not saved, not safe, not with life, but with death. They will be destroyed. It will kill them physically, mentally, emotionally, spiritually. This way of life is the very opposite of what the gospel is meant to produce. The gospel is to produce life – everlasting life – but this way produces death and destruction. This is not the way of regeneration but degeneration.

Thirdly, and I am going back to the Authorized Version here, "Their god is their belly." Pretty blunt phrase, isn't it? But Paul has been blunt throughout this letter. This is a colloquial expression from those days. If somebody said they worshipped their belly, it meant quite simply that bodily comforts, pleasures, appetites and satisfactions came first. Whatever is first in your life is your god. Whatever everything else relates to is central. The god of the belly is the god of the body.

God gave us our bodies in order to live, but where we live *for* the body, we have reversed the order of creation; we have got it all wrong. Thank God for a good appetite. I hope you have a nice dinner today and that you enjoy it. But if your thoughts when we pray in church are, "I wonder if I left the oven on, I hope that meat will be tender," and, "I hope he won't go on too long so it won't be burnt to a frazzle," where is your god? Though the picture is of gluttony, I think it is probably helpful because gluttony is one of the least realised sins of our community. It finds a way right into Christian circles – digging our graves with our knives and forks. But the phrase means more than that. If your prime concern in life is your physical comfort, physical wellbeing, physical satisfaction, physical health, then your god is your belly. Instead of the body serving you, you are serving your body. The body is a good servant but a bad master.

Fourthly, he is teaching: if you follow this through, you finish up with such a perverted sense of moral standards that you turn it on its head and you glory in its shame. You actually boast where you should blush. You are delighted when you should be disgusted. That is one of the side effects of following this through: that in fact, black becomes white and white becomes black and your sense of moral values is lost.

The fifth and final thing Paul teaches is that the mind then gets locked to this planet. Your thoughts never rise above the fridge or the deep freezer. You don't get very warm thoughts usually there. Your thoughts are being tied to the house, to the garden, to the car, to Sunday lunch – none of which things are bad in themselves, and God gave us all things freely to enjoy. But if your mind gets locked in at that level then you really are in a sad condition because you are locking yourself in to things that are going to pass and will be lost. Therefore, what future have you?

With those five simple statements Paul is presenting this challenge: Can you honestly tie that in with the cross? Can you say that that is the life that results from Christ's death?

Christ's death denies every one of those five things. So you are left with the illogical situation of a life that cannot be in any way aligned to Jesus' death at Calvary. But in contrast Paul says to those believers that our citizenship is in heaven. We know that Philippi was a Roman colony. What did that mean? It meant that the people who lived in Philippi had their names registered in Rome. That is where their names were kept and that entitled them to all the rights and privileges of Roman citizenship. So even if they were hundreds of miles away, they would wear the Roman toga to go out shopping, watch the Roman arts at the theatre, go to the Roman stadium to see the sports. A Roman was Roman through and through. You lived that way, you belonged there. Yet Paul is telling them that they are not like those who belong in that place.

In your own life you can see when you look around you that most people's citizenship is here. This is where their interest is; this is how they live; this is where their concerns are.

In every Roman colony there was one great desire: for the Roman emperor to pay a visit. Every colony, sooner or later, had a visit from the emperor, just as Commonwealth countries expect every now and again a visit from the Royal Family. Here is the interesting thing: from the year 48 BC the Roman emperor was given the title "Saviour of Mankind". The greatest day in the life of Philippi or any other colony would be when they heard the trumpet sound and people started shouting, "Our saviour is coming! The saviour of mankind is here!" They rushed out in their Roman dress and they hailed Caesar. "Saviour of the world," they shouted. But Paul says: "We are a colony of heaven, and we await our Saviour." Isn't that interesting? It is a little touch that you could miss when you just read the words. We are Christians, a colony of heaven, and we are waiting for the day when our Saviour is going to visit us. The only person who really deserves the title will get it that day. What will he do for us? When the emperor visited a colony he usually brought some privilege or gift, or some relief from taxes. Something marked his visit that would benefit those to whom he had come. What will Jesus do for us as we await our Saviour in a colony of heaven? It is marvellous news: he is going to give you a new body. He will take this body of our humiliation. I do not find any difficulty in that phrase, do you? Doesn't it drag us low? I wonder how many people reading this wouldn't swap some part of their body if they possibly could. As you look in the mirror, is there anything that you would like to change? Well, it is a body of humiliation in worse ways than that. It is so often through this body that Satan gets hold of us and drags us down. Then we get to an age where we realise this body is letting us down. The eyesight is not so good, we haven't quite as many teeth as we used to have, can't run around with the grandchildren as we thought we might be able to, and it dawns on us that this body is going to humble us. We are going to become weaker and feebler and we will need more help from others. Oh, this body of our humiliation!

This was the thing that rubbed most in Macedonia in Greece where they worshipped the body, where athletics was the great god almost, and where they worshipped the human form. If you study Greek sculpture and art you find that invariably it is men and women in their prime, strong fit bodies – they worshipped the body. Into that situation Paul says, "We await our Saviour who is coming, and he is going to change this body of our humiliation and fashion it according to his glorious body because he has got the dynamite to subject all things to himself." That is the word, "dynamite". Men can only use dynamite to blow people's bodies to bits, but Jesus uses his dynamite to bring them together. His body will be the prototype.

Let me spell that out. I believe that when our Saviour appears I shall have a body thirty-three years old. Hallelujah: a body in its prime! He is going to make my body like his, so he is certainly not going to make me old, and he is going to give me a body that is in perfect submission to the Spirit – so there will be no need to open the door before going through it; a body that could eat fish, and a body that can step out into space. You are going to have a body like that. You see heaven is very physical to the Christian. It is a place, and people have bodies there and we will be able to shake hands in heaven – so much more real than floating nighties and spirits moving around. Heaven is very down to earth in scripture and that is what we are waiting for. We are not people who are saying, "We might as well squeeze every bit of satisfaction and enjoyment out of this body while we can, while we have still got it, and before it gets too old to enjoy it." We have got a new body coming along that will never age and never lose its enjoyment. We will live in the most glorious heaven and earth. What great news that is.

What I believe Paul is teaching here is that Christians live between two physical resurrections: Christ's and their own. The parameters of our thought are the resurrection of Jesus and our own new body coming along when he returns. We live between these two events. But are we so torn between them that we have only to say, "Oh, well that was two thousand years ago and this might be many years hence and so we will just have to sit and wait"? No! What Paul is telling us is that, apart from your body, you can have the rest of your resurrection now. You can live a resurrected life now. You can know the power of his resurrection now. You can live so differently from the people living around you that you know you have obtained the resurrection out from the dead because around us people *are* dead. They are dead in sin; they are dead to God and you can know the resurrection.

For believers the real result in life of receiving the righteousness of God is that you become oriented not to the past which you leave behind you, but to the future which is held ahead of you. You press on for it. You have got ambition to get as much of it now as you possibly can because you can have most of it now. The redemption of your body will have to wait, but the resurrection you can have now; the Spirit who raised Jesus from the dead can quicken your mortal body now. The energy that Christ had when he came out of the tomb can be yours now. The poise and the calm, which had finished Satan, can be yours now. The victory that Jesus had achieved over evil can be yours now.

Please read Philippians 4:1–9

Of all Paul's letters, Philippians is the most personal. He had a closer relationship with this church than with any other that he founded. Of the four chapters in the letter, chapter four is the most personal of all. The first nine verses are concerned with what Paul is doing for them: teaching them, guiding them, correcting them, commanding them, stabilising them, building them up. Then vv. 10–20 are concerned with what they do for him. He ministers to them; they minister to him. He ministers to them spiritually and they reciprocate in a material way, but it is a two-way relationship and that is always a very close one. Your closest friends are those to whom you give and from whom you receive.

So, not surprisingly, in the first verse of his conclusion, he pours out words and phrases which are saying one thing: You just don't know how much you mean to me. He calls them his brothers, which is a miracle for a Pharisee speaking to Gentiles. He calls them "My beloved ones" and only God could have given him that kind of love. I had a lovely letter from a little house group on the other side of the world in New Zealand, where they were using my tapes as a Bible Study. This dear lady wrote, "As we have studied and prayed together week by week, we have become bound together by a really wonderful spirit of love. At first, there were one or two whom I didn't even like." [Isn't that honest?] "But now I can truly say that I love them all and this is the way we feel about one another."

Paul is saying the same thing here. He is telling them

too that they are the source of his happiness. When he is depressed and a little heavy, he sits down and thinks of Philippi and the fellowship there and his heart leaps. He also tells them, "You are my crown." That word is not a crown of reigning but a wreath which was used in the ancient world by holidaymakers and by the ancient athletes when they had won a race and were crowned with such a wreath. He is saying: That is how I feel about you. When I think about you, I have a little holiday inside. When I want to stand before the Lord and be crowned for my work, then I think of you.

All this portrays a very intimate, warm, loving relationship between the apostle and the church. He is very anxious that it should stay that way. So he says, "My concern for you is that you stand firm in the Lord and that I can go on thinking of you this way. Otherwise, instead of it being a joy, it'll be a sorrow. Instead of being my pride, it'll be my shame when I think of you." Indeed, every minister having ministered in a church is very concerned in his heart as to whether what he has sought to do in the grace of God will stand firm. We cannot take that for granted. A church that looks strong and solid and good, as if it will last for a long time, can collapse very quickly. Paul is not complacent, he knows that the Philippians are going to have to stand firm if they are going to go on being his joy and crown.

I once had a very interesting experience. I was invited to go and visit St Paul's Cathedral. I had been there before; I had wandered up the nave and looked at the dome and climbed up to the whispering gallery, and I had fun sending messages around the wall, but this was different. I was invited to go and see St Paul's really from the inside. I arrived there on a beautiful but windy day. The first thing I was asked by a foreman in charge of the renovation of the cathedral was, "Have you a good head for heights?" Out of sheer pride I said yes and regretted it immediately afterwards. He took me up ladders, two hundred and thirty feet, on the outside of the building. After about a hundred feet, I looked down through the rungs and saw little red buses and tiny little specks of people wandering around. My knees turned to jelly and I was anything but standing firm! We climbed to one of the urns on the very top of one of the two western towers. I could see the Hog's Back very clearly. Then I made some extraordinary discoveries. St Paul's Cathedral, to me, has always been such a solid, immovable lump of masonry that it seemed as if nothing could shake that building. Yet, when I got up there, I was shaken rigid. First I could see how the stone was crumbling, how the masonry was cracking all over, and how they needed to pull so much out and replace it quickly before the thing collapsed. I began to feel very unsteady up there. Then I looked down on top of the roof and made a discovery that was astonishing: the outside of St Paul's is not the inside! Did you know that? Those solid walls, with windows and balustrades along the top, are sheer frontage. They don't belong to the building and they are not connected to it. They stand outside it, and there they stand, just a curtain of stone and windows. Inside, further in from either side, is the real cathedral. So the whole thing is just propped up there, or not even linked up. The walls are free-standing and hollow inside. I thought, "Well they could collapse in at any time."

Then I was taken in between the ceiling and the roof. The dome that you see inside is not the inside of the dome that you see outside; the roof is not the ceiling. Going around inside that, there were great cracks on the wall. Stretched over each crack were little electronic instruments stuck to either side with a wire, going to a central place where they can read off how it is shifting. By that time I was wanting to get out of that place. Talk about standing firm! The church was about to collapse any moment! The whole thing is so much on the move, resting as it does on a bed of London clay, that if a water pipe bursts in a street within half a mile, they can read that off the dials of these electronic sensors immediately and ring up the water company and say, "You have a burst water pipe in that street because it's tipping the cathedral." The whole thing seemed so precarious and so much on the move. I was astonished. This great solid-looking building, which looks as if it is there forever, needs constant attention to detail. There is a team of men watching those dials, looking at those cracks, replacing that stone, studying the foundations. Their attention to detail is essential to keeping that cathedral standing. What Paul is doing in Philippians 4 is giving that attention to detail – to the cracks, the foundations, the fabric inside and outside the fellowship – which will help them to stand firm. You can never take a fellowship for granted, however good it is, however strong it appears, however well-established it has been. It is the constant attention to detail that is going to keep it there. Well I hope that picture will help you to get into the feel of what Paul has to say.

There is a pattern to these nine verses. It is not a series of little telegrams of thoughts that occur to him that he just rattles off at the end of a letter. There is a pattern – whether it was clearly in his mind or only known to the Holy Spirit who inspired him I don't know, but the pattern is: watch the details of your relationships with each other; watch the details of your relationship to the Lord, and watch the details of your relationship to yourself. It is constant attention to these details of the building of the fellowship that will keep it standing firm in the Lord.

The first detail that needs careful watching in a fellowship is any cracks in the walls. They are the cracks that appear between people. I remember as a child playing a game in which I would run around the outside of a circle of other children, looking for a gap to try to get inside the circle. Whenever they linked arms tightly, I could not get in. The game was to keep me out. Satan plays that game with every fellowship I know. He is looking for a crack to get in. He will find it when he sees two people who should be arm in arm separating, and that is where he gets in. These are the cracks that need to be watched in the walls of any fellowship.

In the case of Philippi, the crack had come between two leading women. Don't read anything into that at all, it could just as easily have been two men – it simply happened to be these two ladies. I would not like to have been in their shoes when the letter to the Philippians was read out. Paul had the courage needed. He saw something very serious happening and said, "I want you to stand firm." There was a crack in one of the walls and he wanted them to get that crack mended straight away, before it got worse.

There are some very significant points here about how he sets about this. Incidentally, their names in English are Prosperous and Fortunate. Again, I do not know what the significance of that is other than that their mothers hoped they would prosper. They were probably two businesswomen, friends of Lydia. Remember, the church was founded on praying businesswomen, but the crack had appeared. Now look how Paul deals with it and maybe we can learn some lessons here about cracks in churches.

First, he makes it public. It is not a private matter when two of Christ's people are cracking. It is going to affect the whole building. It is not a secret thing, it is something that is affecting the entire structure of fellowship. Paul does not hesitate to name it and to deal with it openly. There must have been quite a hush when the letter was read out, but Paul was prepared for that.

Second, he spoke to both parties. The verb is repeated. He says: I entreat you, Euodia; I entreat you, Syntyche. He works the situation from two ends.

Thirdly, he appeals to them on the right ground, as sisters, family. Now the one thing you cannot do in a family is walk out and join another family. However difficult you find your brothers and sisters – and you didn't choose them in your spiritual family any more than your physical family – you can't say, "Right, I find this family difficult, so I'll move down the road and get into that family."

Fourthly, he realises that they are going to need help and he invites someone to come into that situation and do something about it. People who have cracked from one another invariably need help and encouragement from a third party who can come in, see where the misunderstanding has arisen and what has gone wrong, and help them to get together. So Paul appeals to another person in the congregation: Get in there – help those two to get it together again.

Fifthly, you notice that he says a lot of good about these ladies. How easy it is when trouble has arisen between two in the fellowship, to write them off as being totally bad. But Paul acknowledges that these two have worked for the gospel. They are Paul's colleagues. When he was with the church, they were two he could count on. They had done a lot of good. There is a lovely compassion and sensitivity in saying that they are disagreeing but drawing attention to how much good they had done. It gets the thing in perspective.

Finally, he points out very clearly that God has not written these two ladies off. Their names are in the Lamb's Book of Life. Even if the church wrote them off, God had not done so. Now there is a lovely way of detecting a crack in the wall, getting in there and doing something about it.

Paul is concerned that the Philippians should stand firm and if you are going to stand firm you can only do so together. If Christians cannot bear the sight of each other, they will never face the world.

The second area that he turns to (in vv. 4–7) has to do with our relationship with the Lord – the foundations of the fellowship and cracks there. The first thing that can happen to the foundation of a building is that part of it can sink. Subsidence can bring a building down – depression. Christian books on spiritual depression have been surprisingly popular. Christians can subside. The foundations can give, we can sink and get depressed. It is very important to attend to that and repair it.

There are three things that we are told here about the foundations of our fellowship in the Lord: we are to be a people *enjoying* the Lord, *expecting* the Lord and *entreating* the Lord. Take the first: the Christian will always have something that he can enjoy. Even if everything else is going wrong and even if everyone else has gone, he has got something because he has got the Lord. He can still rejoice in him. The key word here is "Rejoice in the Lord *always*," I find that difficult. There are times when my heart is so full I want to shout "Hallelujah!" There are other times when I do not feel like that one little bit. Sunday night and Monday morning are not always the same experience for Christians. Paul teaches that you have to say this again and again: "Rejoice in the Lord always." He has the victory. We are not to be artificial cheerleaders, but Paul would say that if you are not always finding something to rejoice in the Lord about then there is a crack in the foundations and they are going to subside.

The second thing he says is, "The Lord is at hand." We are to *expect* him. It is going to be tremendous when Jesus comes – with hundreds of millions of people present! What effect does that vivid expectation of his return have on your relationships now? Paul says, "Let your moderation be known to all," or, "Show a gentle attitude to them." There is a Greek word here for which there is no English equivalent and the translators have a real problem. The effect on your relationships of expecting the Lord soon is to introduce this quality which the Authorized Version renders "moderation" – which does not really convey it. It has also been translated "gentle attitude" but there are so many English words you could put in here and they would be right: big-hearted, agreeable, considerate, sweetly reasonable, fair-minded, ready to forgive, unwilling to retaliate. I would say it is the attitude that is willing to give. By that I do not mean giving generously but giving a bit, yielding – an attitude that is not insisting on its rights or its opinions but which knows when to give way, when to back up. It is an attitude that would rather suffer injury than cause it.

The reason why the Lord's coming encourages this is precisely that when you know he is coming soon and that he is going to vindicate you and put everything right, you can afford to be a loser here. You do not need to be afraid to yield or to give. You don't need to fight for your rights; you don't need to be concerned about your reputation. You can yield it because he is coming back, and when he comes back all will be put right. There is a foundation in the fellowship of expecting the Lord to return which will affect our relationships with the world outside. They will know that we are the people who do not mind being losers because Jesus is coming back and we will win.

The third dimension of our foundation in the Lord is to do with worry. We know that worry is silly – it does not add anything to our life. We know that it is sinful. It is unconscious blasphemy. It is saying: God cares more for his pets and his plants in his garden than he does for his children. It is to say that he has lost interest in me. But worry is something that begins to crack the foundations of our trust in the Lord. The cure for it is very obvious. The cure for anxiety is prayer, talking to the Lord about it. Yet many people have found that prayer does not cure worry. They have prayed and prayed about the things they are anxious about. They have poured out their concerns to God and there has been no relief. The reason is that it has not been the right kind of prayer.

There are two essential ingredients of a prayer that is going to reduce anxiety. One is the ingredient of *supplication*. Supplication involves being absolutely specific about what you need. Your worry can invariably be spelt out. If you have a vague feeling of anxiety and worry about the future, get a piece of paper and write down exactly what is worrying you about the future – until you have spelt it out. Then take it to the Lord in supplication, which means, "Lord, please this, and please this, and please this." The cure for anxiety is specific requests in prayer. It is not to pour out a general moan to God that everything is going wrong, but to be specific about the things that are going wrong and what you need. The other thing needed in this kind of prayer is *thanksgiving*. Prayer without thanksgiving is like a bird without wings – it cannot get up to heaven. Thanksgiving not only says, "Please, for this," but also, "Thank you, for that." With this kind of prayer, anxiety goes and entreating the Lord will take away this inroad of worry.

I notice that these three things have to be all-inclusive. We notice if we are to rejoice always, that we are to show our moderation or gentleness to all people, and that we are to give thanks in everything and be anxious about nothing. I do not think you could have more complete advice. The result of these three things – enjoying, expecting, and entreating the Lord – is this: the peace of God acts like a sentry (what a lovely phrase for a garrison town like Philippi) who says, "Who goes there?" If it is something that is going to hurt or to harm you, the sentry says, "Enemy, get away." If it is something that is going to help, the sentry says, "Pass, friend." The peace of God acts like a barrier. When someone's soul has this peace of God, you cannot get beyond it; you can't get through that defence. You cannot shake or disturb it.

The third thing in this passage, vv. 8–9, is our relationship with ourselves. We turn from cracks in the wall and cracks in the foundation to keeping the fabric (inside and outside) under constant renovation. First there is the inside – our mental state. You will have heard this verse so often I hardly need to explain it. There is not a word in it you do not understand: Fill your minds with those things that are good and that deserve praise, things that are true, noble, right, pure, lovely, honourable. There are two great reasons why we find it very difficult to do just this. The first is the world we live in. Our world is not like this. It is a world in which there are many things that could not pass the test of this list. It is a world that presents us with a constant battering of thoughts that are anything but honourable and pure, lovely and of good report. Sometimes I have sat and watched the television news and counted up the different items, then at the end said, "How many of those things were good news and how many were bad news?" It is usually eight or nine out of ten on the bad side. That is the world as we know it.

News media depict a world of everything sensational, bizarre and shocking. These are not the things that God has said we are to keep our minds fixed on. This is not the inside decoration of the people of God.

The other problem we have is this: not only is the world *outside* contrary to this verse, but the world *inside* is too. In my heart and in yours there is a veritable Pandora's Box of things that do not match this test. So what are we going to do? Paul tells us that the way to get wrong thoughts out of your mind is to push right thoughts in. You cannot empty a mind of wrong thoughts just like that. You try to clean out your mind, try to take away those thoughts that are not helpful, and you will find you have got a real struggle. As soon as you get one out, another has come in. Empty the house and clean it up and you will just prepare it for seven more spirits. The answer is to stock the mind with good things. That means consciously exercising a filter so that, when you hear and read, you say, "Now which of these things am I going to keep? Which things am I going to comment on later to other people? Which am I going to meditate about?" So you filter through to your mind those things that are really going to be helpful. You are really saying: What is it that God likes in this situation? What is it that he sees as good? What is it that will be in heaven? Because everything in heaven will be good, pure, lovely and of good report, so I am going to start living now with the kind of mind that I will have when I am in glory, and see those things and think about those things.

Turning from the inside to the outside, not only does Paul command the practice of meditation, but the practice of imitation. He dares to say, "Put into practice what you learned from me and saw in me." I have the feeling that Protestants have been frightened of what the Roman Catholics have done with saints. The result is that we pull away from a source of real help. Right through the ages, in the most unexpected places and circumstances, there have been godly people whose lives you can look at and see Jesus. If we dismiss all the saints, we rob ourselves of a very real source of inspiration.

I heard of a saint called Oliver Plunkett. I am looking forward to meeting him in glory. Who was he? I saw his head in a glass case bound in gold – a skull with a bit of decayed flesh sticking to it. The then pope was kneeling down in front of it. I am afraid my soul reacted against that whole situation. I am quite sure Oliver Plunkett would not have been pleased about it – the whole thing seemed so wrong a use of the saints. But in reacting against that, I find myself if I am not careful, losing the inspiration I could get from Oliver Plunkett. That saint had a school in his own home for Roman Catholic and Protestant children so that they might be one. He paid for it with his life and became a martyr for his faith and love.

You see, the saints are those from whom we learn, not just by what they say but by what we see. All of us, whether we like it or not, model ourselves on other people; we have certain people in our minds who we would love to be like. There is nothing wrong with that, provided you have chosen the right people. Most Christians could give me two or three names of people about whom they would say, "In my Christian life, they are the ones I would most like to be like. They are the ones I've looked at; they are the ones I would love to emulate."

Hebrews 11 portrays for us a gallery of saints – Abraham, Noah, Moses, and the writer goes right through and says, "Look at these men." Then: "But look to Jesus, the author and finisher of our faith..." That is the balance, both for filling our minds with things that are lovely and of good report, and finding the models on which to base our lives. I commend to you reading the lives of saints. It is something that has gone out of practice. There are hundreds of saints through the ages whose lives you could study profitably. This would fill your mind with good thoughts. You would also say in your heart, "They are the kind of people I would love to imitate."

This is repairing the fabric – renovating the structure inside in the thought life, and outside in behaviour. Paul is concerned about this relationship to ourselves. Just as if you get your relationship to God right, then the peace of God comes, so if you get the relationship to yourself right, the God of peace comes, and the God of peace will be with you.

Here then is Paul's picture of a church that is going to stand firm, in which the cracks in the wall are repaired and relationships to each other are right, the cracks in the foundation are put right and the relationship to the Lord is there, so that the peace of God can stand sentry over the fellowship. Thirdly, the people in a church need to be watching the renovation of themselves, inside and out, by the right thoughts and the right models of life.

Whenever Paul says "Stand firm" there is a sniff of battle in the air and you know that he is thinking of war. Perhaps that is why he says so much about peace. One of the photographs I saw in St Paul's, in a little room off the side of one of the galleries, was a photograph of the cathedral in the middle of 1940 during the Blitz. Every building around was down and there were clouds of smoke and flames as London burned after the German raids. Yet there stood St Paul's, solid, firm. Yes, one bomb hit the Quire, but don't read anything into that. The whole structure stood and stayed firm when everything else around was collapsing.

Take that as a picture for my closing word on this passage. Paul is concerned about this fellowship. He loves it, they are dear to him, they are his joy, his pride, but he wants them to last. He senses that there are going to be harder times ahead and his concern is that when everything else collapses, when everything else is being shaken, this structure will stand. So he writes to them in love. They are to watch these repairs, pay constant attention to the cracks and renovate their relationships.

I have a sense that the future in Britain is going to be tougher for the church than it has been for a long time when we had it easy. Nobody interfered with us or opposed us and we have been free to worship. My desire for you is that you stand firm in the Lord.

Please read Philippians 4:10–23

I wonder if you notice in this last section of the letter that Paul seems nervous. There is a certain tension, a sensitivity, an embarrassment creeping in to this final chapter, particularly the second half. He is not quite sure what he wants to say. He keeps expressing fear that he will be misunderstood. He keeps qualifying what he has just said. I have a strong feeling that it is because he is dealing with the question of money. I am not the first to have noticed that Paul found it rather difficult to receive gifts. He was embarrassed by it; he didn't quite know how to cope or quite what to say. I am glad he didn't because he has therefore said much more than he otherwise might, and so put giving to one another in quite a different context, but why the nervousness?

Why, for example, does he say he is glad they have shown their care for him after all that time? He suddenly realises they may take that as a criticism so he indicates that he did not mean they had not been caring for him. Then he says a little later that he did not really need the gift. Then he realises that does not quite sound right so he tells them that now all his needs are met. You find him constantly not quite sure. Indeed, at the end of this passage I could well understand if someone in the church at Philippi had wondered: Well, did he want our gift or didn't he? The answer would be that he did and he didn't.

So let us try to get into this embarrassment. To what is it due? We could find the answer, as some commentators have done, in the Gentile Greek background, where the entertainers were travelling speakers who were always coming out with some novelty. That was the television screen of that era. They were the celebrities of the day and they were on to a good thing. If you could get up and speak about some new philosophy, expound some new idea and then send the hat round, you could make quite a good living at it. Paul was very sensitive lest people might think that he was travelling around Greece preaching the gospel in order that he might make money out of it. Indeed, every preacher where there are large congregations will get that criticism. When Billy Graham came to Britain in 1954 and earlier, there were people who said, "What's he getting out of it? How much does he make?" He had to defend himself on radio and television and show that he did not take one single penny from English people for preaching the gospel here.

In 1 Corinthians 9 Paul says much the same thing, that when he came to Corinth he did not want them to feel that he was charging them or that he was going to live off them. So he deliberately worked with his own hands. He had a trade. Every Jewish rabbi had to have a trade and he simply used his hands to make tents and to make his living that way. Incidentally, notice that Paul did not usually like to "live by faith" in the narrow sense of living by praying to God about his needs and expecting God's people to meet them. He did not like to live that way. He much preferred to be employed and to earn his money.

Is it then simply a sensitivity about what his hearers might think? I don't think so – it goes deeper than that. In 1 Corinthians 9, after establishing his right to be supported by the gospel, after establishing his right to have a wife supported as well as himself, he then says, "Do you think I am going to claim that right? I would rather die first." That is a strong statement. Why is Paul so sensitive? I think we must look for the answer not in the Greek background but in his Jewish background. Paul had been a Pharisee. There are many things we know about the Pharisees but one of them is stated very crudely and bluntly in Luke 16, just after Jesus has been giving some advice about how to handle money. The Pharisees sneered at Jesus because they were lovers of money. They would have sneered: Who does he think he is to tell us how to manage money? He's penniless; he's a business flop. We can handle it. Though the Pharisees were very careful to give a tenth of their money to the Lord, I am afraid their attention was on the nine-tenths. How do I know that Paul himself was trapped in that particular weakness? Well, he says it. Though in Philippians 3 he says, "As touching the law, I was blameless," he only means blameless in the sight of people – they could not fault him on his outward behaviour and observance of the laws. But there was one law that he could not cope with. In Romans 7 he says very frankly that when he read through the Ten Commandments he got to number ten and he could not cope with it. "Thou shall not covet" – when Paul read that commandment he found all manner of covetousness in his heart. Now therefore you can understand why he is nervous at receiving a gift from the Philippians.

It was a considerable gift by the sound of it. It met all his needs for rent, food and clothing for the foreseeable future. He is embarrassed by it because the old Paul did not know how to handle that. Yet he is going to say everything that he does say against that background. He is able to give glory to God and praise God and give a wonderful testimony that this covetous man has been transformed into a contented man. That is one of the miracles of grace that Jesus can perform in a life. A man who was grabbing and wanting, even under the piety of Jewish devotion, has been transformed into someone who can say: I've learned my lesson, I'm content.

You can therefore understand why he lets the Philippians

know it is not so much the gift, it is the giving that really touches his heart. In fact, he talks about anything but the gift itself. We do not even know whether it was money, clothes or whatever. In fact he does everything but send the gift back. In so doing he throws so much light on what really happens when one Christian or group of Christians gives to another part of the Body of Christ, and therefore he initiates us into some lovely secrets.

There are two promises in this last section, which people have quoted and treasured for years but which so often they have taken out of context and therefore misinterpreted. If you have got one lesson from these studies in Philippians I hope it is this: always study the context. Always put a text in its context or you will treat it as a pretext, and this applies to both promises here. Promise number one, "I can do all things through Christ who strengthens me." What does that mean? We tend to claim it when we have got a big task ahead, when we have some big achievement awaiting us and we say: "I'm capable of anything through Christ who strengthens me."

But put it back into context and it is a promise given to those in impoverished circumstances. If we add one word to the promise we shall get the meaning more accurately: I can do *without* all things through Christ who strengthens me. That is a different promise, isn't it? The strength he gives is the strength to do without – that is the promise. If you take it out of its context you apply it to Christian service and Christian achievement whereas in fact it relates to impoverished circumstances.

Take another promise: "My God will supply all your need according to his riches in glory in Christ Jesus." You think "great" – until you put it in context. In the context, that promise is given to those who have impoverished themselves to supply the needs of others. Then the promise comes: and my God will look after you. If you are impoverished in your circumstances, you can claim: "I can do all things through Christ." If you have impoverished yourself to help someone else then you can claim, "My God will supply my needs according to his riches." You can see that it is very important to get right into a passage.

We now look at three things: first, what this gift really meant to Paul; second, what it really meant to the Philippians; third, what this gift really meant to God. Here are the three dimensions when any money changes hands within the Body of Christ. It means different things to the giver, the receiver and God.

First of all, then, to Paul himself. He says: It has made me very happy in the Lord; I enjoy God more since I received your gift than I did before; I am happier with him now that you have given something to me. That is an insight in itself and we must ask why this gift made his relationship to God more enjoyable. Why has it deepened his happiness in the Lord? The first reason he gives is that it has conveyed their concern to him. You don't really know how much people care for you until they do something about it. They may have been caring all along, yet it is when they express it that you know they do. Unusually, Paul uses a metaphor from horticulture. He rarely talks about things in nature. Jesus talked about nature a lot, but Paul's illustrations come from the big city – from sport or from business. Here he is saying: "After all this time your concern, your care, has flowered again" – that is the word he uses. Have you had a plant in your garden that has just done nothing for three or four years? Then suddenly you have gone around the garden, then you have come back in and said, "You know that plant? It's flowering again, it's still alive. It's still got the power to produce flowers." Paul got that kind of thrill. When this gift arrived from the Philippians he realised that what had been lying dormant was still alive, and they still cared, and they were still concerned. That is always a thrill. He had to correct it, as I have remarked, because he might have given them the impression that he felt they had neglected him, which he did not feel. But to think that the flower of care had been there all the time and was now bursting into blossom again after all these years – it came as a great thrill in prison to know that they still cared. Maybe that might touch you to express your care shortly for someone towards whom you have not expressed it for a long time, just to tell them it is still there and it is flowering again for you. That would bring a great thrill.

Secondly, Paul says that this gift confirmed his contentment. He had learned one of life's biggest lessons. It is a lesson that very few learn, and it is something that has to be learnt because it does not come naturally. Contentment must never be confused with a placid temperament. Contentment is something you either learn or you do not learn. You are not born with it. We are born with its opposite – we want more and more. It is natural to be covetous; it is not natural to be content. Socrates was once asked, "Who is the wealthiest man on earth?" His reply was, "The man who is content with the least."

Wealth is not measured by your bank balance; it is measured by how much you want. The two greatest tests of contentment are if you find yourself with too much and if you find yourself with too little. Both conditions are examinations in the school of life to see whether you have learnt to be content. Paul is saying: I've learned it, I've got the lesson. So he says, in effect: I didn't need your gift. If it hadn't come I wouldn't have asked for it, I wouldn't have prayed for it, I wouldn't have wanted it. I'm perfectly happy with what I have. Now for a covetous man to be able to say that is a tribute to the sheer transforming friendship of Jesus Christ.

Let me highlight just three little phrases: I learned, I know,

I can – they come in that order. By "I learned" he doesn't mean I *am* learning. It is a verb that means "I learned it once for all, I have learned my lesson, I will never have to learn it again. I am past that; I am through that class. I have moved up and I have passed both exams. Indeed, he uses some pagan religious language to express this. He says, "I've been initiated into the secret." There were many pagan mystery religions which talked in that kind of way, about people who had been initiated into their secrets, much the same way as Freemasons today talk about being initiated into the mysteries of Freemasonry.

Paul is saying that he has been initiated into the secrets of contentment. Then he says, "I know". You cannot be initiated unless you are able to say that. It means "I know firsthand." You can only learn this if you have known what it is to have too little and if you have also known what it is to have too much. Probably you have not known both. But if you have then you will have discovered whether you learned the secret. You have got to go through both classes in God's school if you are really to learn this secret. Therefore Paul says, "I can". What is the secret? It can be explained very simply. It is to learn how to live on your inner resources instead of your outer resources. It is a very deep secret and it is imparted only to those who really know Jesus Christ personally, in secret. Let us spell this out very practically. When you are in a situation where you have too little, then the inner resources you need are literal, physical strength to keep going. Do you believe that you can draw that inner strength from Jesus when you haven't the food to supply the outer strength? Jesus knew he had that – six weeks he was in the wilderness without food.

I lived in northeast England in the 1930s and I can remember the depression, the needs, the poverty that there was there. But one of the testimonies I heard as a boy has stayed with me vividly. It keeps coming back to me. I have never been in this situation myself but the testimony was so strong. It came from an elderly retired fisherman in a little village on the Northumberland coast. He told of how, in the days before social welfare, one Christmas day he opened his little pantry and all there was in it was one crust of dry bread.

Dear old Peter (I don't know his surname) said, "I took that crust of bread and I broke it in half, and put half back for Boxing Day, and I sat down to my Christmas dinner and thanked Jesus for it." Then he said, "You know, after I'd eaten it I felt I'd had turkey, plum pudding, the lot." And he did – you could see it – and he did not eat anything for the rest of the day. I will never forget the impression that made on my young heart. He was a man who could feed on Jesus, quite literally, for his Christmas dinner. It was so real, so practical. Paul is saying that he has learned how to do that.

When you are in a situation where you have too much, that is as much a test of your contentment as when you have too little. Let me quote a little phrase which I am afraid I may have used from time to time, and daresay you may have: "Well I really oughtn't to, but it is so nice, thank you so much." Have you ever said that? Then you have not passed the test of having too much. If you need physical strength from Jesus inside when you have too little, you need moral and spiritual strength when you have too much, lest it take hold of you. I wonder which is the more difficult – to be content with too little or content with too much. Both are severe, acid tests and I believe this promise, this secret, which Paul now outlines, is going to be needed more and more by Christians. I see no other future for us but one in which we have too little compared with what we have had. Now what is going to happen? When we had too much, did we learn the secret of being content? Far from it, we are now a nation of malcontents. What a testimony it would be if, when things get tighter, Christians are genuinely able to say, "I've been initiated into the secret. I can do without through Christ who strengthens me. I have inner resources to live on." So closely connected are body and spirit that it is literally true that your body can live on your spirit, just as things that happen to the body also affect the spirit.

Do you remember how once when Jesus and the disciples were pretty hungry, hot and tired, the disciples went off to get some food, and Jesus talked to a woman? He asked her for a drink of water, which he never got. She was so interested in what he said that she never bothered to give him the water. When the disciples returned, Jesus was not hungry. Why not? He had meat to eat that they did not know about. There is a real sense in which the spiritual and the physical appetites are related. The inner resources and the outer resources are not totally independent of each other.

Paul is teaching that this is the secret: whether I have got too much or too little, I don't live on what I have got outside, I live on what I have got inside; I have learned the secret so, even though your gift was welcome, I could have managed perfectly well without it and I was managing perfectly well without it. Not a very nice way to say thank you, but nevertheless it was an honest testimony from a man who had once been just the opposite. So to put the matter right a little he had to correct it.

One man who really found an anchor for his soul here was Oliver Cromwell. When he lost his only son, it was a tragic break in his life. He felt the bottom of his world had dropped out, and he went through a real emotional crisis. He asked the Lord to give him a word that would hold him through the crisis and this is the word the Lord gave him: "I can do all things through Christ who strengthens me." So he was able to take that promise and say, "I can do without my son through Christ who strengthens me." He was using it in the right sense: I can do *without* through Christ. I have got enough inside to cope with whatever is taken away outside.

So Paul then goes on to say that the gift to him meant that it covered his commitments. I sometimes think it was a little easier perhaps for Paul because he was unmarried and did not have a family. That always adds to a person's sense of responsibility and therefore anxiety. But nevertheless, even though he was an unmarried student in the school of experience, he learned his lesson. But he did say thank you for their sending the gift. "I've got more than enough" – in other words he is saying, "Don't send any more, all my needs are met." In all this I think Paul is not looking at the outside of the gift but the inside of it. It means concern from them and it means contentment in him.

Now he turns to what the gift means to the Philippians. In an extraordinary way, he talks in commercial business language and does not use the language of charity. But the church at Philippi was founded by a businesswoman, and when you give to another part of the Body of Christ that is not charity. It is first of all an investment of their capital. It makes them shareholders. When you invest money in a Christian you have become a shareholder in that Christian. It is not as if having given a bit of money it has gone and is now nothing to do with you – out of sight, out of mind. It is not like that in God's sight. In his sight, your gift to that person is your investment (see v. 15).

It is an intriguing phrase and I sometimes wonder why they were the only ones. I have the feeling it was because Paul would not let the others help. I may be wrong but he would not receive help from Corinth, for example. I have the feeling that he made an exception here. He writes: "You had fellowship with me." That means: You became partners in my profits and losses – if my business made a profit, you would share it; if my business made a loss, you would share it. He was thankful that when he left them he could recall that, more than once, when he moved on to Thessalonica they did not say, "Right, that's Paul gone and out of sight, out of mind – now we'll get on with the business of being a church here." No, they wanted to be partners in that business, wanted to share his work. So they sent a gift again and again. It was not so much a gift as buying shares in his business. That is an extraordinary thing to say but he says it very clearly here. So he is not only saying "It was good of you", but: It was good for you to give; you have made a good investment.

Which brings me to the second thing—not only was it an investment of their capital but it would bring interest to their credit. He makes no bones about this: You became partners so that if I had a loss you would have it; if I had a profit you would have it. Paul wanted to tell them we have made a profit – it was not a loss to them. Even though in financial terms they had lost money, they had gained credit, a profit. They were not out of pocket; they had in fact got something to their credit because God is going to audit their accounts.

Heavenly accounts work in the opposite way to earthly ones. What you spend on others is a loss to an earthly account but it is a credit to a heavenly account. It is investing treasure in heaven where moth and rust do not consume. That is what Jesus was trying to tell the crowds in Luke 16 when the Pharisees sneered. He taught them to use their money to make friends who will welcome you in heaven, and who will say, "I'm so glad you spent that money in that way because here we are in heaven as a result." Jesus was teaching: That is how to invest your money to get the best returns, with no inflation, no loss, no decline. The Pharisees sneered and said that he did not know how to handle money, but he did know.

Paul is telling the Philippians they have made a good investment and will get interest. So he covets their gifts – not for himself but for them. He wants them to go on giving, yet he did not want to go on receiving. It is all part of this tension within his soul. The message is: I've got more than enough but please go on giving – I want you to get credit to your account. So according to the Greek he actually sends a receipt (v. 18 has the technical word in the Greek language for "paid in full") so he is saying, "Here is my receipt – more than enough; paid in full.

Now at this point you might begin to think that this is a bit of a reciprocal trade agreement and that I am playing on very wrong motives. Some tele-evangelists are criticised for deliberately appealing to this motive, saying, "If you give to me, you'll get more than you give back again from God." In other words: you are on to a financial winner if you give to my campaigns. People do jump to the wrong conclusions so quickly. Paul saying that it is an investment for which you are going to get interest – immediately people could get the wrong idea.

My grandfather, when he was a minister at Bakewell, once went to Chatsworth House, knocked on the door and asked to see the Duke of Devonshire. When he met him he said, "I've come to offer you the best investment you've ever been offered." He was wanting funds for something for the Methodist Church in Bakewell, and he had the face to do it! Maybe that is where I get a bit of it but he went right up to this man and said, "Here's the best investment in the bank of heaven – certain interest." I think he went away with quite a substantial gift. Should we be appealing to that kind of motive? Is it simply a commercial transaction? To stop anyone jumping in purely as an investment, Paul lifts it to a much higher level. Another party is involved in this – God. You can't transfer money from one pocket to another without God noticing. Do you remember when Jesus sat over against the treasury watching what people put in the collection? Do you realise that Jesus will watch what you put in the collection too? He is interested to see whether it is simply an offering or whether it is a sacrifice. There is a difference. So Paul turns now to what this gift would mean to God. The underlying assumption is that whatever you do for one of God's children you do for God. Every parent knows that is true. If someone is kind to your child they are kind to you – and you feel grateful.

God is involved in our lives and our transactions. What does he feel about a gift that is transferred from one part of the Body to another? There are two things that Paul says. First, it is a smell he will appreciate. The gift of smell is one of the most lovely gifts, I think. You would have no taste if you had no sense of smell. A few unfortunate people lose their ability to smell permanently and eating is like eating cardboard, and that must be a terrible trial. I have been blessed with quite an acute sense of smell but I find it a great joy. Fried onions is one of my favourite aromas. I remember as a child sniffing the tar laid on a newly tarred road. Does that get you? Or the smell of woodland after it has rained. Do you know that smell when it seems to release something fresh? There are all kinds of smells that are lovely, and there are others which are horrible. The Bible often talks about God as if he were human. It talks about his eyes, his mouth, his ears, his hands, his arms, his legs, his bowels, and it talks about his nostrils – not because God has a body, but there is nothing that we can do with a body that God cannot do without one. Therefore all the senses we have God has as well, but without the organs of sense. Difficult for us to imagine, but it means that God is not denied the pleasures that we have. For example, do you think God would have created so many flowers with a beautiful scent if he could not smell them? Do you think that he doesn't enjoy smelling flowers? Of course he does. God told the Jews that there was one smell he did like and it was the smell of roast lamb. I am putting this in a very down to earth way but when they wanted to give God pleasure they took a lamb and roasted it totally, turned it all into smell so that God could smell and say, "Roast lamb this Sabbath", and it would give him pleasure. That was a burnt offering to God, deliberately designed to appeal to his sense of smell.

Now when people meet each other's needs because they are God's children and because of their love for one another, that smells right to him. It releases something within the atmosphere that smells good to him. So Paul does not hesitate to say this. Then he goes on to say one other thing – it is a sacrifice God can accept. If I brought a lamb to church, lit a fire and cooked the meat, then said, "God, smell roast lamb," he could say: No, that's not what I wanted – in offering it you have shown that you have not understood what I have asked for. Since Jesus, you don't need to do that; it is not acceptable any more.

I am rather relieved it isn't, because the temple must have been a bit of an abattoir when they were sacrificing thousands of lambs, goats and bulls. I am glad we don't have the kind of bloody mess which there must have been in Old Testament days. We should find it quite offensive and off-putting. God has given Jesus – so the old sacrifices are not acceptable any more. But there are sacrifices which are. Presenting your body a living sacrifice is acceptable to God. Giving of your material possessions to someone else is acceptable as a sacrifice. There are sacrifices that are inappropriate now to God, that are not acceptable, which could give him pain rather than pleasure. If we tried to offer him a lamb for our sins it would be an insult to his Son, the Lamb of God who takes away the sins of the world. But there are sacrifices that are acceptable and Paul is explaining that it was an act of worship when they met his needs – not just an offering but a sacrifice.

One characteristic of a genuine sacrifice is that it has really cost the donor something. When they brought a lamb to God in the Old Testament it was not the weakest lamb in the flock but the strongest – the best, not the worst. It was the firstborn, not the last born. It was not what was left over, it was the very first thing, and the best they could find, without blemish and without spot. A sacrifice had to be worth something to the one giving and that is why Jesus said of that widow, "Did you see that widow making her offering?" That offering was a sacrifice. In church we usually say, "The stewards will now wait upon you for your offerings." I think it is just plain honesty that prevents us from saying, "The stewards will now wait upon you for your sacrifices." Do you see why you cannot use the words interchangeably?

Paul is saying something here about the Philippians. He knew that it had cost them something. They had done without in order that he should do with. He has confidence that God will supply all their needs, looking after them. "My God will go on supplying" is in the present continuous tense, which means he won't just do it once – he will go on doing this. Let us get the flavour of that phrase "according to his riches". It does not mean *out of* his riches, it means *in proportion to* his riches. He will do it as the wealthy multimillionaire he is. That is the way God supplies needs – "pressed down, shaken together, and running over". Nobody can ever accuse God of being niggardly. No-one can get God in their debt because God would not allow that – it would allow people to patronise him if we could say, "I've given more to his people than he's ever given to me." God will not let that happen.

A church member wrote down their testimony, headed, "Whatever he says to you, do it" –

During the member's meeting, in which it was decided to go forward with the building of the church extension,

I was very much challenged by the appeal for the money to meet the cost of it. On that evening, the Lord told me definitely that he wanted my wife and I to give a certain sum. When I got home I told her, and it was the largest sum we had ever been challenged to give at any one time to his work. We thought about it, yet the Lord reminded us that this was the amount he wanted. After several weeks the decision came, and a cheque was made out for the amount, put in an envelope and placed in the offering on a Sunday morning. Two days later, the exact amount of money came back to us from a source we knew very little about. Five weeks later the Lord has repaid us three times over. We praise the Lord for all his love.

At the bottom was written "The Lord repays with interest." Isn't that a lovely little testimony? Not because whatever you give to the Lord he will give three times the amount back within five weeks, though that is a pretty good rate of interest when you work it out! The reason he gave that back was that the gift was *not* given for that purpose, nor for that reason or from that motive. If nothing had come back it would still have been given.

Indeed, God knows what we need. It says, "My God will supply all your need." It doesn't say, "My God will supply all your greed." Therefore, if you don't need money back he won't give you money back but he will supply the other needs – according to his wealth in glory. He has enough wealth on earth, all the silver and the gold is his and the cattle on a thousand hills are his – but what is the wealth in glory like? That is how he will repay, and he has banked it all in the name of Christ Jesus. All his riches in glory are in Christ Jesus – in his name. So if you want to tap those resources you will need to get his name on the cheque. You will need to be able to say, "In the name of the Lord Jesus," and then you can cash the cheque. No wonder Paul bursts into: "Glory be to our God and Father...." Not just *my* God now, but *our* God. He is the God who takes responsibility for us – he has underwritten us. We belong to him and we are his children.

So we come to the very last three verses, the greetings at the end of the letter. When we end our letters with greetings such as "Yours sincerely", "Yours faithfully", "Yours truly", etc., it may be a formality, but Paul puts in Christian greetings here which are a very important part of Christian living. We are the members of the Body of Christ – with the different organs, but vital to a body's health is the circulation. If that is not right, the organs will not function. The circulation in the Body of Christ is the circulation of love. But that can be too vague and general. It expresses itself in the circulation of things like gifts and greetings – gifts moving around the Body, greetings moving around the Body – and greetings are very important. Paul includes such a lot of them at the end of this letter.

Greetings to all the saints in Philippi, greetings from my brothers here, greetings from all the Christians here, and even greetings from those in the imperial household. Incidentally notice that the word "household" is not the word "family". That should help you when you come to household baptisms but the "household" is the same as the Queen's Household Calvary. It means the servants – from the lowest menial to the highest functionary. It is amazing that Paul's incarceration in the imperial prison meant that people in the imperial household now knew Christ. From the palace they were being prepared for the mansions in glory and they sent their greetings. So Paul passes on greetings from them, and there is a circulation of greetings.

Why is Paul so keen to do this? Greetings do four things for us. First of all, if you greet someone you are acknowledging them as a person. That is why I have sometimes heard people say, "Well I went to that church and no-one spoke to me." They have a right to say that. They are saying: "Their love was not enough to recognise me as a person. Oh, they pushed a plate in front of me for the collection, but no-one spoke to me." Greetings acknowledge a person. I am a terror for this: my mind can be miles away and I can walk right past someone I know, and I am aware later that it has hurt them because I did not greet them.

Secondly, greeting is reinforcing that relationship. Every time you say hello to someone, your relationship is just a little bit deeper than it was before.

A third thing a greeting does is to express concern for someone. We used to say, "How do you do?" Nowadays people often say, "How are you?" I don't recommend answering that honestly because people are quite bothered and don't quite know what to do. Even to say goodbye is to say "God be with you," which is what it is short for, and that is expressing a concern.

Finally, a greeting seeks the wellbeing of the person you are greeting. It is saying, "I want you to be blessed; I want you to be better supplied than you are now; I want you to have good health; I want you to know real life." "Shalom" is a lovely greeting you can use. It means "I want you to be at peace, I want you to have harmony with yourself, with others, with God." So these are all the reasons for greeting and that is why in church services we often greet one another as well as bringing our gifts. They are both part of the circulation of the Body, a sweet smell to God and a sacrifice acceptable to him.

This is a very deep and personal letter and it finishes with this lovely greeting, the best thing of all. What could I really desire for you? What is the best greeting you could give somebody? It is: "The grace of the Lord Jesus be with you all." It means the generosity of the Lord Jesus, the grace of the Lord Jesus who though he was rich yet for our sakes became poor, gave it all away for us. May the grace of the Lord Jesus be with you.

For more of David Pawson's teaching,
including DVDs and CDs, go to
www.davidpawson.com

FOR FREE DOWNLOADS
www.davidpawson.org